sanctuary

Creating a Blessed Place
to Live and Love

Pamela J. Bailey

D0030557

Walk Worthy Press

West Bloomfield, Michigan

WARNER BOOKS

NEW YORK   BOSTON

If you purchase this book without a cover you should be aware that this book may have been stolen property and reported as "unsold and destroyed" to the publisher. In such case neither the author nor the publisher has received any payment for this "stripped book."

Epigraph on p. 94 comes from *Principles of P*, by Annie Tyson Jett, copyright © 1998. (Self-published)

Copyright © 2006 by Pamela J. Bailey
All rights reserved.

Published by Warner Books with Walk Worthy Press™

Warner Books

Time Warner Book Group
1271 Avenue of the Americas, New York, NY 10020

Walk Worthy Press
33290 West Fourteen Mile Road, #482, West Bloomfield, MI 48322

Visit our Web sites at www.twbookmark.com and www.walkworthypress.net.

Printed in the United States of America

First Edition: May 2006
10 9 8 7 6 5 4 3 2 1

Library of Congress Cataloging-in-Publication Data

Bailey, Pamela J.
   Sanctuary : creating a blessed place to live and love / Pamela J. Bailey.—1st ed.
      p. cm.
   ISBN 0-446-69516-5
   1. Christian life—Christianity. 2. Home—Religious aspects—Christianity.
3. Sacred space. I. Title.
   BV4501.3.B343 2006
   248.4—dc22   2005022206

Book design and text composition by Giorgetta Bell McRee

*This book is dedicated in loving memory to my father,
Lawrence Randolph Campbell, who told me that
I could do or be anything and assured me that the world
was bigger than my own neighborhood.*

*To my mother, Eunice Campbell, from whose well of wisdom
and strength I continue to dip and fill my cup.*

*To the families whose loved ones were lost and whose lives,
families, and homes were changed forever on
September 11, 2001.*

Contents

Preface: Discovering My Sanctuary   vii

Introduction: A House or a Home?
How to Use This Book   1

Principle ONE:
Seek God for Wisdom and Guidance   5

Principle TWO:
Understand Your Home History   13

Principle THREE:
God Responds to Excellence and Gratitude   23

Principle FOUR:
Make Your Home Your Family's Haven   35

Principle FIVE:
Love People and Use Things   49

Principle SIX:
Permeate Your Home with Spirituality   59

Principle SEVEN:
Consciously Set the Emotional Tone of Your Home   71

Principle EIGHT:
Create an Atmosphere of Comfort and Joy   83

Principle NINE:
Use Your Home as a Place to Relax and Rejuvenate   93

Principle TEN:
Personalize Your Space   103

Principle ELEVEN:
Have a Charitable Home   113

Principle TWELVE:
Build on a Foundation of Integrity   123

Principle THIRTEEN:
Stand Guard at the Gate and Be Careful Who Enters   133

Principle FOURTEEN:
Celebrate   143

Afterword   149

Acknowledgments   151

Reading Group Guide   153

About the Author   160

Preface

Discovering My Sanctuary

*I*t never ceases to amaze me how the smallest, sometimes seemingly insignificant, things can inspire the heart and create awe at the many wonders of God. That is exactly how this book and the philosophy that now drives my attitude and perception of *home* were conceived.

Many years ago, my husband and I made a bold and arduous decision to sell our newly built home located in a beautiful new development. We moved to an older, smaller home in a town nearly thirty miles away from the fast-paced metropolitan city where we were living. This decision was a difficult one, not only because it was our first home, but because I had been able to decorate the interior with beautiful and expensive things. Two major events then ensued to influence our decision to sell the house and move.

The first event was the demise of our small business. In addition to each of us having full-time careers, my husband and I owned and operated a service-oriented business. Because of budget cuts and overall tightening-of-the-belt by the companies we were servicing, we subsequently lost valuable contracts, which led to closing our business. The second and most important event, however, was the birth of our son, Braeden. We decided that it had become increasingly difficult to have valuable family time together because we, like millions of other families, were caught in the cycle of newer, bigger, better *things* at the expense of a fulfilling home life. We were forced to work harder and longer hours to support our lifestyle. Our commitment to our son and to one another became our motivation to sell our house and put more focus on our family.

After living in a small, cramped apartment for nearly a year, we finally purchased a nearly fifty-year-old ranch-style home in a quaint neighborhood very reminiscent of the town where I grew up. The older home had good bones, a beautiful established yard, and many interior features that I could appreciate. However, though I liked our newly purchased home, I remained unattached and uncommitted to it. It did not have many of the features that our first home possessed, such as three bathrooms and all new appliances. This house had only one bathroom, no dishwasher, and a stove that must have been original to the house. During the first nine months of living there, I couldn't even decide on a paint color for a single room. Then something simple and yet extraordinary happened.

My husband and I decided one weekend to thin out a natural area in our side yard so we could appreciate the magnolia trees, dogwoods, and ivy-covered pine trees that grew there. As I began to pull up weeds and cut back vines, I stumbled on a tiny woody object on the ground and lay down my tools so I could examine it more closely. It was an abandoned bird's nest that had fallen to the ground. But it was much more than that! Some little bird had taken tiny bits of nothingness and created, by sheer instinct, a refuge for her family. Holding that nest in my hand and viewing it with great scrutiny, I saw how the bird had skillfully and painstakingly woven straw, twigs, leaves, and a few small golden strands—probably remnants of holiday tinsel—together to create this exquisite home.

It was the place where she fed her family, encouraged them, and ultimately, taught them to soar. As I began to look more closely at the nest, I became awestruck, excited, ashamed, and inspired all at once. Were these not the same goals that I aspired to in creating a home for my family? Had Jesus not declared that as God cared for the fowls of the air, he would care for me also, only more? I recognized then that He had also supplied me with everything I needed to create my own refuge, my sanctuary. Instantly, I was humbled and grateful.

I thought (and, in some instances, rightfully so) that some family and friends would think less of me because my home appeared to be less than what they expected of me. But I quickly grasped that I was substituting my house for my own self-worth. I also realized that newer, bigger, and better had somehow translated in my mind to mean more successful, happier, and more important.

I had forgotten that even though my first home had been beautifully furnished, none of those *things* were special or held any significant meaning for me. Frankly, I found them boring. For my husband and I, none of those possessions held any history or connection to our families in any way. I had not perused any quaint shops waiting patiently for the perfect piece that said "me," nor had I *created* any one piece that gave me a sense of accomplishment. Even the pictures and paintings on the walls were purchased more for color coordination rather than inspired pieces of artwork from a favored artist who spoke to my soul.

I began to examine how we were living in our new home. With limited space and another child on the way, were we using our home to the best of its function and ability? Had I made sure that I was creating a place where my family could be comfortable and constructing an environment that my children would cherish for the rest of their lives?

Home became for me, at that very instant, a place to create lifelong memories with my family. Later, with the addition of my second child, Brinn Elizabeth, it became birthday party central. I made a decision that our home— our nest—would be a place filled with love and laughter and people who wanted to share in our lives. Armed with greater appreciation and a deeper understanding of myself, I set out to create my very own blessed home.

As I share my story and these principles with you, I encourage you to look more deeply into your connection to your own home. Ten different interior designers can decorate the same space in ten different ways, but none of them have a real sense of who you are unless *you* truly know who you are. It doesn't matter at all whether you own or rent, whether you live in a palace, a tin-roofed cabin, a trailer, or a historically registered antebellum mansion; home is truly where the spirit rests and the heart resides, and it should be treated with the greatest respect, sincerity, and love.

Author's note: Some of the names and details of the stories about friends shared in this book have been changed in consideration of their privacy.

Now therefore let it please thee to bless the house of thy servant, that it may be before thee for ever: for thou *blessest, O Lord, and it shall be blessed forever.*

KING DAVID
1 Chronicles 17:27

Introduction

A House or a Home?
How to Use This Book

*I*f asked to define the words *house* and *home*, many people would say there is little difference between the two. The words are usually used interchangeably when people describe the place where they were raised as children, or the new condominium they have just purchased. However, distinct differences exist between a house and a true home.

A house, for instance, is a building, constructed of a variety of substances like brick and mortar, concrete blocks and stucco, wood and nails. Many similarities are consistent in all houses regardless of the building materials, location, or square footage of the house. For example, every house has a roof, windows, floors, and a front door. It can be a stand-alone dwelling surrounded by a yard and garden or an apartment within a building that contains hundreds of units. But, it is merely a piece of property that can be bought, sold, or inherited. A house is a house whether any one resides in it or not. It can be completely devoid of all life, no family and no furnishings, and still be a house. An aesthetically beautiful house can sometimes also give the false impression that it is the equivalent of a good home.

A home, however, is something much more. Unlike a house, whose value is usually determined by the neighborhood where it sits or the number of bedrooms and bathrooms it has, a home's intrinsic value is made up of the intangible things that cannot be determined by amenities. A home is a living, breathing entity that is created with and sustained by memories, family, gratitude, style, joy, respect, love, godliness, cleanliness, time, celebration, and appreciation. The list can go on and on. With godly wisdom and deliberate effort from a home's inhabitants, these amenities are obtainable by all who choose to acquire them. Ironically, they are all things that in terms of dollars and cents cost nothing.

Likewise, such things as fear, addiction, disrespect, ungodliness, abuse, infidelity, uncleanliness, and dishonesty can destroy a home and wreak havoc in the lives of the people who live there. Intentionally or not, a home is a reflection of the person or people who reside in it.

The Bible is a valuable tool for creating a spiritually beautiful atmosphere in your home. How we live in our homes *is* important to God, so much so, that Proverbs 3:33 tells us that the Lord curses the house of the wicked, but He blesses the homes of the just. Some of us have inherited a legacy of a blessed home, but far too many of us have pain and negative experiences interwoven in the fabric of our home experiences. Although we cannot rewrite the histories that many of us have lived within our past homes, we each have the ability to create beautiful, spiritual, and peaceful home environments of our own, beginning today.

It is important to examine your own home with an honest eye. Choose to look beyond the obvious—the material things that you possess or lack—to the substantive value of the choices you make about your living space. The following principles will help you evaluate your current living environment and consciously create a blessed space where you and your family can flourish. Use the Home Work exercises to help you see your home in a new light. Make your house a sanctuary by following the principles to create a loving and a more spiritual space for you and your family to enjoy. Be blessed!

Principle ONE

Seek God for Wisdom and Guidance

Today, I will call upon the Lord and I will seek the wisdom of God in the decisions I make concerning my home. I will create a blessed home.

Except the Lord build the house, they labor in vain that build it.

PSALM 127

Seeking the wisdom of God is the first and the most important decision one can make in creating a blessed home. Where will I live? Is it time to buy? Will this person make a good roommate for me? Should I live near family or move away from family? These important life-changing decisions should be done only after seeking direction from the Lord.

An enormous amount of creativity and skill goes into the design of a house. The architect, the builder, and the interior designer all work together to build a functional living space with skills and expertise they each have obtained through seeking a higher level of knowledge concerning home building.

We, too, have the ability to obtain a greater knowledge beyond that which we already possess. The Bible encourages us to "seek God in all our ways." God's wisdom, as we see throughout the book of Exodus, is infinitely more than book knowledge. This wisdom is referred to in the Scriptures as "wisdom of the heart." It means being inwardly moved or motivated to do and be your best while following the lead of the Lord.

God gave Moses detailed instructions about how to build and furnish the Sacred Tent and told him whom he should use among the people of Israel to do so. In Exodus 35:30, Moses told the children of Israel that the Lord had called Bezaleel by name and He had filled him with the spirit of God, in wisdom, in understanding, and in knowledge to create special works for the house of God. The Lord gave Moses the knowledge to select every cup and vessel, design each praise garment, and select the jewels and every yard of fine linen used in the Sanctuary. The children of Israel performed the work as God had commanded it of Moses.

Wisdom of the heart transcends common knowledge. It allows us to create sacred environments that are beyond anything we could create on our own merit.

How can we apply this concept to our own sanctuaries? God will stir up our hearts and allow us to live excellently and in abundance within our own homes if we are willing to do the following:

Pray for guidance in our homes. Luke 18:1 says that we should always pray. It stands to reason that since we cannot be in church all the time because we work, raise families, and go about our daily lives, home plays an important role in our praise and prayer lives.

Listen and wait for instruction. Our flesh often causes us to act too quickly. We make decisions about staying put or leaving our homes because we are angry, hurt, or frustrated. We sometimes move into living situations that are not pleasing to God and are contrary to His word. It may be God's will that we seek another home, but His timing is impeccable. He may very well be setting you up to obtain great things, but if you move too quickly, you may miss God's intended blessing for you.

Be willing and obedient to the word of the Lord. Sometimes God chooses to bless us in radical ways. He will instruct us to move out of our comfort zones—perhaps a neighborhood where we grew up or the city where we have family close by. Genesis 12:1 shows us how God instructed Abram to get out of his country and away from his family to go to a place that God would show him. With this move to a new home, God promised Abram he would be blessed beyond measure. Acting on faith, Abram departed as the Lord had told him to do and as he journeyed along the way, he prayed and called upon the name of the Lord. Consequently, God gave Abram a home greater than Abram could see with the naked eye. Along with the land came the oath that it would belong to Abram and his seed forever.

Malachi and Gwen were faced with a similar decision to stay in a place where they were quite comfortable and complacent, or make a radical move to be obedient to the will of God. Malachi, a Philadelphia native, had worked in the ministry for many years faithfully assisting other pastors. Then one day God let Malachi know that it was time for him to pastor his own church. This new church would be located in North Carolina, away from the family and friends who would so easily support him in a new work. But, God wanted him out of his comfort zone.

Malachi sought God for wisdom through prayer and fasting. Then he put out a fleece before the Lord, asking Him for confirmation before he uprooted his wife and children from the city where they had lived their entire lives.

Malachi knew how important their home was to his wife. In the year that they owned their home, she had designed a warm and wonderful environment. She oversaw every detail—even directing the landscaping crew as they strategically placed every shrub and flower in their yard. Gwen knew her husband's history with God, so when Malachi confided to her God's plan for their lives, she trusted that whatever he was led to do would be the right decision for their family.

This decision, however, did not come without opposition. First, the couple learned from the real estate agent that their home had not appreciated in value in the one year they had owned it. If the agent was successfully able to sell their home, the bank would get the bulk of the proceeds and they would still owe the agent for thousands of dollars in commission fees. Then, Malachi traveled to the city that would be their new home to look for work only to find the prospects were grim. Ironically, he had just been promoted on his old job and now as he was preparing to move to North Carolina, job opportunities in Philadelphia began to pour in. Still he remained strong in his resolve and prepared his family for the move.

He accepted a job in North Carolina at just slightly more than half of his previous salary. He moved his family to a small and crowded apartment, reassuring his wife that whatever they sacrificed for the ministry, God would reward them many times over. One evening they got a telephone call from their real estate agent in Philadelphia. Knowing the family's mission to birth a ministry, the agent was calling them to forgive the nearly four-thousand-dollar commission fee that was owed to him. "You are such good people," he said. "I am sure you can use that money for the new church, so I am tearing up the bill."

After laboring to build the ministry for more than a year, the couple decided to buy a new home. As they began their search, Gwen wandered into a great neighborhood; there sat a beautiful house in the middle of a large corner lot, and it had recently been placed on the market for sale. It was grander and more spacious than the home that she left behind. The fenced backyard would be the perfect place for the children to romp around.

As a formality, she looked throughout the city for suitable houses, but she always came back to this one. When she contacted the seller's agent to inquire about the selling price, she soon realized that the home was way out of their price range, but she remembered her husband's words about God rewarding obedience many times over. So, undaunted by the high asking price, Gwen began to drive by the home daily. She would park in front of the house and pray about it. Finally, she made an appointment with the agent to see the home. Once inside, she knew that *this* house had to be hers.

As they continued their search, Gwen secretly claimed the home that she had already found as their own. In her mind, she plotted out the new landscaping design. She imagined the children's rooms painted in colorful hues, selected to match their individual personalities. She sketched out ideas for new draperies and window-shopped for new furniture that would fit perfectly into the upstairs nook between the family's bedrooms.

Then the homeowner suddenly took a job in another city and was anxious to sell the house so that he could purchase another. Able to negotiate the contract within their price range, Gwen and Malachi moved into the home of their dreams.

- Acknowledge that you do not have the answers to every problem and situation that may arise in your home.
- Keep in mind that there is no challenge too hard or too small for God. Ask Him to give you wisdom when you are making decisions about major investments like a

home. There may be hidden things that you are not privy to, such as troubles within a neighborhood or undetected structural problems in the foundation of the home. There is also the possibility He may help you obtain a home in a different way than you ever imagined. You may learn about the perfect apartment community from a friend or coworker, or you may choose to buy a home through a real estate auction or a bank foreclosure. You may be blessed to finance your dream home in ways other than traditional lending institutions, or God may provide a way to pay off your mortgage without a loan and own it outright.

- Know who is really the head of your house. You may pay the bills and select the furniture, but know that God is in total control. Learn to relax and rest in Him.
- Finally, be willing to accept what God allows. Be open to whatever answers He gives you, even when they seem to put you at a disadvantage. The Bible tells us that "the steps of a righteous man are ordered by the Lord."

David loved King Saul. Saul, however, feared him because God was with him. David behaved himself wisely when he was in the king's home. As Saul's son-in-law, David lived among the king's riches with many servants at his disposal. Yet there was no peace for him in that home.

Saul's heart was not right toward David, and he unjustly sought to kill the brave warrior while he lay asleep in his bed. God used the king's own children to warn David and later aid him in his escape from Saul's home and his wrath.

God may sometimes make things around you so uncomfortable that you have no other choice than to seek Him in finding and creating your own blessed home.

Home Work

Make a list of concerns about which you are seeking guidance for in your home.

1. _____

2. _____

3. _____

4. _____

What kinds of things can you consciously do to remind yourself to seek the wisdom of God in your home (e.g., placing your Bible out on a reading table or next to your favorite chair rather than tucking it away in a drawer)?

_____

_____

Find an enjoyable way to make seeking God's wisdom a normal part of your daily routine. For example, try reading your Bible while you sip your evening cup of tea or before an early morning jog. What other things can you do to connect seeking wisdom with the idea of enjoyment?

_____

_____

In all things give thanks. Thank God for at least one thing about your home environment every day!

Principle TWO

Understand Your Home History

Today, I will revisit my past home experiences and determine how they influence my present-day home decisions.

*If a house is to be set in order, one cannot begin
with the present; he must begin with the past.*
                                JOHN HOPE FRANKLIN

*E*ven as God was bringing the Israelites out of captivity, they murmured and complained. They confided to Moses that their bondage in Egypt was somehow more bearable than a challenging journey into a Promised Land flowing with milk and honey. A history of abuse and bondage by Pharaoh, coupled with fear of the unknown, actually made captivity seem attractive to a blessed people. When we make decisions about how and where we choose to live, we should explore our own home histories to see which elements of that history influence our decisions and our ability to fully enjoy the homes with which God has blessed us.

Before you buy one more piece of furniture or hang another picture, you must first do your Home Work. Believe it or not, how you choose to beautify your environment or even the fact that you may choose not to do so may be a great indicator of what is manifesting in your spiritual and emotional life. I am a firm believer that everything in our existence runs full circle and our feelings about ourselves manifest in every aspect of our life, especially our homes. We need to examine this concept closely to understand more deeply the relationship of how we see ourselves and how we live in our environment. Every choice we make, even about simple things like paint color or how we will use the rooms of our homes, is driven by something deeper than the obvious.

For example, I can often easily gauge the emotional and spiritual status of my own life by simply looking around my home and reading its cues. If I am handling most challenges in my daily life but have some issues I wish to avoid, my home is usually neat and tidy except for one corner of a room or a desk that is filled with clutter. The clutter undoubtedly is indicative of the avoidance of cleaning up issues in my personal life. Doing your Home Work may result in your being a better steward over your home. The Home Work exercises can help you clear your emotional clutter to make way for more spiritual growth. You even may gain the courage to create an intimate space—a unique haven that is special to you. Having a separate, sacred space in your home will provide a quiet spot for prayer.

Most of us have some emotional issues, and if we look closely, we can see them manifested in some way in our homes. The following are just a few examples of a relationship between our inner turmoil and our surroundings:

1. You love color but are afraid to use it in the paint or furnishings in your home. You may:
   - have a fear of putting yourself on display to face possible criticism.
   - value the opinions of others more than your own.
   - be afraid to make mistakes and/or accept responsibility for mistakes.
   - be reluctant to take emotional ownership of your space.

2. You are afraid to enjoy and fully use your home and furnishings. You may:
   - harbor fears that you will not be able to acquire more wonderful and beautiful things in your home/life should these get damaged or become worn.
   - have feelings of unworthiness and think you don't deserve beautiful things.
   - feel you must keep up an appearance of perfection in your life.
   - feel you will be judged by others based on your material possessions.

3. You are afraid to seek help in making choices or changes in your home. You may:
   - fear appearing vulnerable.
   - believe people will not think you are smart or capable if you can't decorate perfectly.
   - be afraid to commit to your choices, or dislike being put into a position of having to make a decision for which you will be held accountable.

4. You are constantly shopping and buying things to fill an already cluttered home. You may:
   - feel unfulfilled, empty, or dissatisfied with your life.
   - be avoiding painful issues in your life and do "feel good" things to temporarily bandage emotional hurts.
   - have an unorganized and cluttered life filled with unnecessary baggage that you are either unwilling or unable to unload.

5. You are living in a home that you cannot really afford. You may:
   - be overcompensating for a financially poor childhood.

- be attempting to compensate for low self-esteem and self-worth by living above your means.
- lack integrity and be willing to risk your financial future to receive praise or envy from others.

When my husband, Ray, and I were newlyweds, we lived in several apartments before buying our first home. No matter what was the layout of each apartment, I always chose—without much input from him—to decorate in shades of the color green. Hunter green was always the predominant color in my living and dining spaces. I never gave it much thought. I chose furnishings, accessories, and wallpaper with that underlying color scheme because somehow it felt right to me. It wasn't until we were building our first house and making design choices with our builder that my husband asked me to consider choosing a different color palette. "Sure," I said, but somehow we ended up with green marble countertops, hunter green upholstered dining chairs, and green exterior window shutters and front entry door.

A few years later I was sharing a fond early childhood memory with Ray about my family's life in New York City, when a picture of our apartment there flashed in my head. In an instant, I was transported back to my parents' beautifully decorated living room with its velvety soft green sofa. *Hmm*, I thought, *this is interesting*. Having lived in three different homes throughout my childhood, I began to reflect on each of them. Although I couldn't remember many of the details within the handsomely pine-paneled living room of our second home, the intricate designs in the green floral curtains were crystal clear in my mind. And the last house I shared with my parents before creating a home with my husband had—you guessed it—living room walls, sofas, and curtains all in various shades of green.

Was that a revelation for me! I was using familiar colors very much the way many people often use comfort foods. Because I was in a new relationship with new expectations from someone whom I was still getting to know, I was subconsciously holding on to something from my past that made me feel at ease. This wasn't necessarily a negative thing, except I was still creating a "me"-centered environment rather than attempting to create a "we"-centered one. This is an interesting phenomenon that affects just as many men as women. Think about how often men lament over missing their mother's special recipe or how they think laundry should be folded exactly the way Mother used to fold it. There are probably a million and one ways to fold a towel, but often such trivial peculiarities with regard to our homes carry emotional weight from our pasts. That's why understanding our emotional home history is so important for our spiritual growth as individuals.

Take Sandra for instance. She is an accomplished businesswoman, well traveled, and collects artwork and antiques from all around the world. In her business life, Sandra is organized and decisive, but her home is cluttered with her acquisitions. She dresses in bold colors and ethnic prints, but the walls of her home are the same "new house" white they were when she first bought the place. Her beloved paintings sit on the floor, leaning against the walls, and most of her treasured first edition books are still packed away in boxes. For years family and friends have offered to help her get settled in, but she has always refused their offers of assistance. Her income could easily pay for a top-notch interior designer, but Sandra doesn't see a reason to rush her decorating decisions.

Sandra was raised as a military kid. Her father's high-ranking position forced her family to move often. It always seemed to her that just when they were about to become acclimated to their new home, her dad would receive orders to ship out to another base with his family in tow. Sandra's mom had finally gotten to the point of never fully unpacking or hanging pictures on the wall because they were always preparing for their next move.

Although Sandra has not lived with her parents for nearly twenty years, and has owned her own home for more than six years, she is still stuck in her military kid mode. She is unable to make a commitment to her own home because her past has taught her that she should be prepared to move at any time.

Too often we allow the spirit of fear to rule how we live in our homes. The fear of cutting old ties, the fear of being held accountable for our decisions, or even the fear of instability caused by early life experiences can limit our enjoyment of our homes. No matter what your particular limitations are, they are all based in fear.

Sarah and Abraham of the Old Testament allowed their fear to create problems in their home. Although they had many amazing experiences with God, their home history was one that was initially steeped in fear. Twice it was nearly torn apart because Abraham feared for his life and told both Pharaoh, King of Egypt, and Abimelech, King of Gerar, that Sarah was his sister and gave her to both these kings to wed. Abraham was such a blessed man that God troubled the homes of these great kings on his behalf, both times interceding and returning Sarah back to her own home.

Then Sarah allowed her feelings of fear and inadequacy for never having had a child with Abraham to influence her decisions and rule her home. Her lack of confidence in God and in herself caused her to upset the peace of her home when she asked Abraham to conceive a child with Hagar her handmaiden. Sarah's fear later brought grief and anguish into her life, forcing Abraham and his first-born, Ishmael, son of Hagar, to permanently part from one another.

Fear is caused by a lack of faith and we are told in 2 Timothy 1:7 that God has not given us the spirit of fear but He has given us the spirit of love, power, and a sound mind. If we are willing to trust God in all things, we can live freely, independent of our fears in the special places we call home.

Home Work

Write it down! Revisit your childhood home in your memory and write down five things you loved about it. Now recall and write down five things that you wished were different about it.

FIVE THINGS I LOVED	FIVE THINGS I WISHED WERE DIFFERENT
1._____	1._____
2._____	2._____
3._____	3._____
4._____	4._____
5._____	5._____

What things have you consciously or unconsciously repeated in your home from your past home experiences (paint colors, styles of furnishings, habits, attitudes)?

_____

_____

_____

_____

What things can you do today to clean up your emotional issues and help create a more spiritual space?

_____

_____

_____

_____

Principle THREE

God Responds to Excellence and Gratitude

Today, I will give thanks to God for my shelter. I will treat my home with the respect that it deserves and strive for excellence in how I live in it.

Daniel was preferred above the presidents and princes, because an excellent spirit was with him.

DANIEL 6:3

Sometimes our present home environments may not be exactly what we had envisioned. When I first moved to Charlotte, North Carolina, many years ago, that was the case for me. In my final months of college, my father died suddenly from a massive heart attack. After graduation I moved back to my family home to deal with my grief. A childhood acquaintance, who was already living in Charlotte, graciously invited me to move into her home until I could get my bearings and begin a new life as a career woman with my new degree in hand. Eager to escape the pain of losing my father, I jumped at the opportunity to leave my hometown and the familiar to move to a place that held the promise of new experiences and possibilities.

I felt certain this move to a new city and a new home would afford me the kind of Mary Tyler Moore-hat-tossing excitement that I daydreamed about in my college marketing statistics classes. The truth of the matter was I was not prepared to be in anyone else's space. I was still reeling from the shock and hurt at my father's passing. Finally, the living arrangement became uncomfortable for my friend and me, so I moved out in an effort to salvage our friendship.

Having been on my commission sales job for only a few months, I was not financially prepared to rent my own apartment. I was faced with the decision of moving back home or staying in a city that I quickly had come to love. I chose to do the latter and moved into the YWCA. The day that I lugged my belongings into that tiny room with cinderblock walls and a narrow slit of a window, I sat on the built-in bed and wept for hours.

I wept because I barely had enough space in that room to change my mind. I cried because the room was too drab and claustrophobic. I shouted, kicked, and screamed because I had just lost my daddy, someone I loved as much as my own life. I hollered because I was scared and all alone in a strange space in a new city without the security of my family and my family home.

Then one day I was sitting on the sofa out in the common area on my floor at the YWCA watching television with four new residents who had just moved in to the facility. As we began to introduce ourselves and share our stories, I learned that three of the women were recovering addicts being housed at the YWCA because of the overflow of clients at a nearby drug rehabilitation center. They were undergoing intensive counseling, their last phase of treatment before being reintroduced into the world of sobriety.

As they candidly shared their painful stories of how past hurts, abuses, and neglect had brought them to the point of addiction and now recovery, I felt as if God had sent them to this place, at this time, for me. I needed to understand *that I was blessed right where I was!* My challenges paled in comparison to the real-life drama that these women had lived through. For them this place represented cleanliness, freedom, and a second chance.

I decided at that moment, even if for a brief period,

this would be my sanctuary. The next day I went out and bought myself the plumpest down comforter set that I could afford. I added scented candles and an artsy but inexpensive floor lamp and an area rug. I lined my dresser with pictures of my family and friends, the people whom I loved most. Instead of lamenting my stay in this place, I began to think of my little room as a suite in a swanky hotel. After all, the YWCA had a gym, a pool, and great restaurants within walking distance.

I became grateful to God for giving me a comfortable and warm place to stay. I was blessed to have encountered these women who were so willing to be open and honest with a stranger about their own lives. I was grateful to the friend who had shared her space and supported me in creating my own. I quit complaining and canceled the pity party. I decided to be excellent and show God my appreciation for what He had allowed, and within another month, I was moving out of the YWCA and into my first leased apartment.

Maybe you want to own your own home but for now you must rent. Perhaps you envision a larger home or one in a better neighborhood. Remember, God knows and sees all: our innermost thoughts, our outward actions, and the desires of our hearts. We must learn to be excellent in all of our ways and be thankful for what God has presently given us so that He can entrust us with future blessings. The Bible tells us that when we are faithful over a few things, He will bless us with more.

Consider the story of Joseph, the son of Jacob, in the Book of Genesis. Joseph was suddenly and violently snatched from his childhood home—a comfortable and wealthy place—and thrown into a pit by his eleven older brothers because he had found favor with his father. Merely a victim of circumstances, he was sold into servitude into Potiphar's house. Potiphar was the captain of the guard over Pharaoh's army. Joseph took excellent care of Potiphar's home and impressed his master so much that he was promoted to oversee all that Potiphar owned.

Like Joseph, we sometimes lose the home we love because of circumstances seemingly beyond our control. Divorce may force us to sell the home we thought we would live in for the remainder of our lives. Sometimes the death of a spouse, illness, or loss of a job can force us from the places we love and cherish the absolute most. Even in those instances, however, we must exhibit the faithfulness and appreciation that Joseph displayed. We should always be aware that the omnipotent God will take care of us if we trust Him. Matthew 6:32 says that your heavenly father knows your need for all things. When we are grateful and we strive for excellence, God will honor what is special to us.

Joseph respected Potiphar's home and refused to disgrace it in any manner. When he refused the sexual advances of Potiphar's wife, she devised a plan to have him thrown into prison, truly one of the most uncomfortable places anyone could call home. Even in prison, Joseph knew God could bless him in that environment so he performed his prison tasks to the best of his ability and he triumphed. He took a potentially unbearable and possibly deadly living condition and acted in such a godly, respectable fashion that he began to gain favor with his captors. Eventually the keeper of the prison believed that he could put Joseph in charge of anything and that Joseph would do it well without supervision.

Later, the king's home became Joseph's home. Because Joseph never complained, but always made the best of whatever circumstances he found himself in, God allowed him to be a ruler over all of Egypt. The former servant was now blessed in such abundance that his own great home was eventually filled with servants to do his bidding. God had used Joseph's experiences to enable him to go higher and higher, to grow more spiritually, and financially to live better than he ever could have had he remained in his father's house.

Certainly, Joseph had a grateful perspective and the spirit of excellence, and God saw that and it pleased Him. A grateful perspective is the key to seeing the glass half full rather than half empty. Gratitude transforms the typical into the unique and the mundane into the extraordinary.

Alice, a dear friend, often reminds me of how important it is to be grateful in your home. She has vivid memories of being raised along with ten other siblings in a rural South Carolina town. Their little house was hardly capable of comfortably providing what most would consider adequate shelter. Still, Alice is grateful. She recalls having to light a candle to find her way to the outhouse in the middle of the night. She remembers cold winter nights when she and her sisters held their blankets in front of the wood-burning stove to warm themselves and then made a mad dash to their bed to preserve the heat as they lay three, and sometimes four, in one bed.

Under such seemingly primitive circumstances, Alice's mother showed her family tremendous strength and love. She instilled in Alice a strong sense of independence and self-reliance, nurtured her musical talents, and taught her to be an incredible cook on that wood-burning stove. Living in such tight quarters demanded a strict daily routine of cleaning and organizing. Alice has become highly skilled at both.

Recently, Alice shared with me how she is able to look back on the time of her youth with such appreciation. Though it is difficult to fathom how such hardship could be held with great fondness, every memory for Alice is a marker for how far she has come and how blessed she continues to be. She thinks about that outhouse as she is cleaning one of the three bathrooms in her present home, and she openly gives God praise. She does not mind vacuuming her carpets, remembering the rough-hewn wide-plank boards of her childhood home that she once swept with a homemade broom of straw gathered from a nearby field. Without a doubt, she has a greater appreciation for the simple pleasures of home that many take for granted.

Be sure to show gratitude to God for your home today. Whether it is more or less than your childhood home, whether it is more or less than you've expected, be filled with gratitude. Keep Joseph in mind and know that you, too, can go from a prison to a palace or back to a prison again—unless your actions are excellent in the eyes of God.

Most of us know how to ask God for things we are lacking. Here are some ways to be grateful!

• Appreciate the value of having shelter. Give thanks every single day that you have a place to call home, no matter how humble or elaborate your home may be.

Even if your temporary home is a room in a boarding-house, take ownership of it and treat it in a way that is pleasing to God!

- Spend less time dwelling on your future home or dream house and be grateful for the present blessings, the "right here" and "right now."
- Choose to decorate your space as beautifully as your budget will allow. Start small, if necessary, acquiring one item at a time like a lamp, a rug, or a cozy bed comforter.

Show respect for yourself and your family by maintaining a physically and emotionally "safe" home environment.

- Have older homes and apartments, those built before 1970, tested for lead levels and other potential hazards that could cause serious illness in young children.
- Change inside air filters monthly to allow good quality air to circulate in your home.
- Invest in an air purifier if you or a family member suffer with allergies or if you live in an urban area where air pollutants are a common problem.
- Be conscious of fabrics, fibers, and chemicals that can cause skin irritations or aggravate allergies. Encourage your immediate family to leave their shoes at the door to prevent bringing outside chemicals and pollutants into your home.
- Add an inexpensive water filter to your kitchen faucet to get rid of impurities that may be in your tap water.

Just as He cares for us, care for the home that God has entrusted to you.

- Don't let unfinished projects linger around your home. Doing so can lead to feelings of frustration that result in nothing being accomplished. Start and finish one project at a time. Don't delve into a new project until you are completely satisfied with the first. When your budget allows, hire a handyman or barter your skills with someone who can use your help on his or her home improvement projects.

- Take a class at a home improvement store. These classes are usually free to attend and you can learn such skills as laying floor tile, faux painting techniques, and installing light fixtures. Local community colleges offer low-cost workshops that teach valuable home-maintenance skills and provide an opportunity for hands-on experience.

- Men, especially, need to understand that taking care of projects in other people's spaces before accomplishing tasks at home can be a great source of ill feelings and dissension. It is a wonderful thing to want to help others; however, Mom, the boss, and your buddy must all get in line behind your spouse's needs for home repairs. After all, her home is your home too.

- Be sure to give your own living environment the kind of respect and caring that you would give to the most expensive home in your community if you owned it.

James is what some in his trade call a "carpenter's carpenter." As a third-generation craftsman, his woodworking skills garnered him some of the most sought-after jobs in the home restoration business. He could quickly rattle off the addresses of homes in the local historic district that had been brought from various states of disrepair to their now regal appearance as a result of his handiwork. Unfortunately, James never had that kind of enthusiasm when it came to caring for his own home.

Paint peeled from the clapboard siding, the sink in the hall bathroom leaked, and the front porch was piled high with found parts and salvaged things that James had promised to use to do repairs when he found the time. Ruth, his wife, was always frustrated and embarrassed about the condition of their home. She stopped entertaining and inviting friends over to dinner several years ago. When they first married, Ruth had envisioned their lives together in this cozy home surrounded by a manicured lawn and a cutting garden out back, but James had never taken an interest in his own home the way he had in homes of his well-to-do clients. Because his work was seasonal, and thus their income unreliable, Ruth had never been able to hire someone else to do repairs and complete James's numerous unfinished projects. To add insult to injury, James would quickly respond to neighbors and family members whenever someone needed him to fix something or make repairs in their homes.

Finally, after Ruth threatened to leave, the two sought counseling to try to understand how their individual life experiences had manifested in how they cared for their current home. James's father, who had also been a skilled carpenter, was extremely frugal and always denied James's mother's request to honor their home by making it the best it could be. On weekends, his father would load the family up in the car after church to drive by the latest grand home he had helped to refurbish. James remembered vividly his father's response when the children would dream out loud about one day owning fine homes like the ones they'd seen on their Sunday drives. His father's tone was always discouraging. He would tell them, "People like us don't need fine homes like that." James had therefore never thought himself worthy of the best, and how he treated the things and people that were near and dear to him reflected that sentiment. Ruth had seen James's attitude as not loving her enough to give her his best. She felt neglected and cheated by his reluctance to care for their home. Fortunately, through counseling, the couple was able to work through their issues and restore their lost respect for their home and for one another.

Seek excellence and respect in your home, not just in the material objects found there but in the way you treat everything the Lord has entrusted to you. Begin each day prayerfully and with gratitude. Here is an example of a prayer I use to honor my space.

A Prayer of Excellence

Lord, make me excellent in all my ways. I confess that there are things I do not know, was not taught, or did not see in my childhood home. But, Lord, in the home that I choose to create, please help me to know what is best so that I may dwell in it, in a way that is pleasing and acceptable unto You. Show me Your ways, O Lord, and teach me Your paths. Lead me in truth and teach me and I will be forever grateful to You. I will be careful to give You all the honor, all the glory, and all the praise. Amen.

Home Work

Walk through your home and find some detail in each room that you appreciate. If there is no such feature, create it!

_____

_____

_____

_____

_____

_____

Honor your home by fixing what is broken or damaged. Look around your home; make a short list of what needs to be repaired or replaced. Decide on a reasonable time to have the list completed, then begin a new list until all repairs are done.

_____

_____

_____

_____

_____

_____

_____

Principle FOUR

Make Your Home
Your Family's Haven

Today, I will make my family's comfort a priority in our home. I will encourage their input and share ownership in the decision making for our home. I will acknowledge that cleanliness inspires clarity and clutter creates chaos. There is no room for chaos in a blessed home.

*She looketh well to the ways of her household,
and eateth not the ways of idleness. Her children arise up and call her blessed.*

PROVERBS 31:27–28

*F*or me, making my home a family haven, clean and
comfortable, is somewhat of a mild obsession. Nothing
thrills me more than my family's eagerness to return
home after a long activity-filled day, or even from an enjoyable vacation. I try to bring truth to Dorothy's time-
honored statement from *The Wizard of Oz:* "There's no
place like home."

The Bible gives us the example of the phenomenal
woman in Proverbs 31. This woman is concerned about
her household. She brings food from afar. Just imagine
the meals prepared in her home with exotic herbs and
spices. She rises in the wee hours of the morning to prepare food for her household, ensuring that even her servants are fed well and provided for properly. She assesses
their needs to be assured that everything is in order before she leaves her lovely home.

She doesn't worry about the snow because she has
clothed her household in the best apparel. She goes to
great lengths to make her home a place of elegance and
comfort.

Proverbs 31:27 says that she "looks well to the ways
of her household and eats not the bread of idleness."
Translation: She is not at home watching her soap operas
or chatting on the phone when her house is a wreck. Inevitably, her children will call her blessed and her hus-

36

band will praise her. An added bonus I'm sure, is that she will undoubtedly feel pretty good about herself, too.

My own mother taught me the value of basic home comforts, including good food, cleanliness, and aesthetic, well-made furniture, as the interior foundational building blocks for a desirable home, but my dear friend, Ramona, taught me to make comfort and luxury in the home a real priority.

I was introduced to Ramona in her home many years ago when Ray, then my fiancé, insisted that I meet and get to know her. He knew that the positive attitude and God-centeredness that he had experienced over the years as her godson would benefit our relationship and me personally. I immediately found her comforting, refreshing, and un-pretentious, and her home reflected every one of those virtues. Ramona has learned over the years how to create intimate spaces throughout her home at very little ex-pense. She recycles yard sale and thrift store chairs and re-stores them to their original glory—overstuffing them and then reupholstering them in beautiful carefree fabrics. Her similarly acquired collection of miniature lamps adds ambience to every room, giving each a blissful coziness.

Because her home is small, Ramona makes every inch of space count. Her guestroom does extra duty as a den and computer workroom. Everything in her home gets used, from the cobalt blue stemware in the kitchen to the reproduction Hepplewhite chest in the living room that is used for storage. Upholstered footstools and benches are scattered throughout for quick, portable seating, and miniature tables serve as decorative and utilitarian sur-faces. Closets store homemade quilts and buttery-soft throws that make napping a decadent experience.

Ramona gives great attention to detail. Beside the bed is a pitcher and glass set filled with ice water to quench the thirst of a guest in the middle of a warm summer's night. High-count cotton sheets, large thirsty bath towels, and plumply stuffed pillows make visitors wish they never had to leave her home. The atmosphere of Ramona's home is calming and peaceful. Even her front porch with its rockers, topiaries, and blooming plants beckons passersby to stop and relax for a while. Each of us should be able to create a comfortable environment that honors our spirit and expresses our gratitude, no matter what our budget. Here are a few suggestions to achieve this goal:

- Invest in furnishings that are functional and comfortable. These elements are as high a priority as beauty.

- Give special attention to detail in the areas of your home that your family will use intimately and routinely. Comfortable mattresses are important for you and extremely important to growing children. It is believed that a good night's rest or lack of one greatly affects our attitudes and levels of productivity.

- Use your furnishings' budget first in areas that are the most beneficial to the people who live in the home all of the time. Plump pillows and great sheets are of far greater value to a family than an expensive dining room suite that is used only when relatives visit during holidays and special occasions.

- Dress your home in the manner you would dress yourself. You would not buy an expensive suit to wear over torn and tattered undergarments. Likewise, you should not buy unnecessary expensive furnishings before you stock your linen closet with plush towels.

- Make furnishings flexible by attaching wheels to chairs, tables, and ottomans so they can be moved easily from room to room.
- Remember that paint is the easiest and most inexpensive way to inject warmth and personality into your home's interior and exterior spaces.
- Honor your children by giving each of them input in his or her own space. Let your children help decide on the decorating choices in their bedroom and playroom spaces. It is a great way to begin to give value to their opinions and help them develop confidence in their own choices.
- Involve everyone in decision making to help each family member feel home is a true haven for them. Dispense age-appropriate information and allow everyone to have input in decisions that affect the family. Doing so instills a sense of pride and ownership in those decisions.

Clean it up!

A clean environment is the foundation for creating a blessed space for yourself and for your family. This is probably the most obvious and controversial issue in many homes today. It is an idea that is simplistic, and yet the importance of cleanliness escapes so many people, regardless of the size or value of their home. We have numerous reasons and excuses why our homes are not properly cared for, many of which involve time, money, or energy. Compound these excuses by careers and extracurricular activities, and our homes become extremely neglected spaces.

Living in a severely cluttered or an unclean home can

deeply affect our attitudes, moods, and spirits. Children who live in unclean and cluttered environments can suffer from depression-like moods and often live in shame. A clean home, even if it is sparsely furnished, can be uplifting and delightful. As we read in the previous chapters, it is important to understand why we have clutter as well as why it is important to take care of our homes first.

I have to admit that when I began conducting workshops for Christian organizations to teach about home and family concerns, I was truly shocked to find that cleanliness, or the lack thereof, was a huge problem in many homes. As a matter of fact, following financial disagreements, cleaning issues are always second on the list of household challenges.

Before we examine what the Word of God says about maintaining the home, allow me to share these points for your consideration:

• Know that cleaning and maintaining the home is the responsibility of everyone who resides in it. No one, including men and children, are excluded from this obligation. In fact, most children, by the age of three, can regularly participate in an age-appropriate way in the upkeep of their homes. It is up to a home's occupants to decide who will perform which tasks.

• Be aware that wives and moms are not called by God to be maids. There is absolutely no reason why a grown man who can navigate his own way to work every day should have such great difficulty carrying his own underwear to the dirty clothes hamper or placing a glass in the dishwasher. Many men do care about the condition of their homes and are willing to clean and maintain it, too. Many parents do a great disservice to their sons by not teaching them how to care for the home at an early age.

• Get help! There is no shame in hiring a professional or a maid service to clean your home. Working moms and stay-at-home moms alike need to optimize the time they spend with their families, so do not feel guilty if your budget allows for hired help. If not, spend quality family time together performing housekeeping duties.

Now that said, let us examine what the Bible *does* say about a woman and her home. Titus 2:6 instructs the older women of the church to teach the younger women to be faithful keepers of the home. In Genesis, God required that Adam and Eve maintain the Garden of Eden, their home, to keep it beautiful and well groomed.

As Christian women, we sometimes completely miss the boat. We think that going to church a couple of times each week and serving on a committee is all we need do to please God. Granted, these things are important in developing and maintaining a relationship with God; however, they are not the extent of our charge. God cares about every aspect of our lives. Even how we live in our homes.

Mark and Rhonda had been married for nearly nine years when he decided that he had simply had enough of living in a filthy home. His job in pharmaceutical sales allowed them to live a comfortable middle-class existence. Rhonda had worked as a legal secretary until two years into the marriage, when she became pregnant with their son and opted to stay at home with him. Mark worked long hours, and mounting sales quotas made work stressful. Many evenings he came home to a messy and cluttered home. Mark understood that caring for their son was indeed a full-time job for Rhonda, so he vacuumed, put away dishes, did laundry, and never complained. Unfortunately, on one income, they could not afford to hire someone to help, so he just did what he could to keep the home clean and organized.

Rhonda decided not to return to work after their son started preschool, so Mark assumed that with much of her time freed up Rhonda would take more interest and responsibility in the maintenance of their home. However, quite to the contrary, Rhonda used her newfound time to chat on the telephone with her family, go clothes shopping, hang out with girlfriends, and catch up on her sleep. Dishes were constantly piled in the kitchen sink and old newspapers were strewn across the coffee table in the living room. The laundry hamper was always overflowing, and little piles of clothes sat in the corners of every bedroom in the house. The kitchen floors were sticky because months went by between moppings, and the carpets were dirty and soiled. Several containers of food had become unrecognizable mold-covered globs in their refrigerator. After countless verbal sparring matches between the two and Rhonda's declaration that "she did not have to do housework if she chose not to because she had better things to do," Mark sadly packed up his and their son's belongings and moved out of their home. He promised to return to share a home with Rhonda only if she decided to accept some responsibility and treat their sacred space with more respect.

Eventually Rhonda and Mark reconciled. They agreed that having a home together was important to them, and once they established a routine, making home a clean, sacred space became easier. What Mark and Rhonda realized was that establishing a routine is essential to maintaining a clean home. Think of your routine as "power cleaning."

Although a clean home is an optimal environment, this does not mean you need to be a slave to your house. The power-clean strategy is one that establishes a maintenance routine for your home. Your power-clean schedule might look something like this:

- Set aside an hour on two separate days each week to clean and sanitize your kitchen and bathrooms. Keep handy disposable disinfecting pop-up wipes in your bathroom and kitchen areas for quick cleaning. This will help reduce illness caused by germs in your most commonly shared spaces.
- Take forty-five minutes, once a week, to dust, change bed linens, and fluff your living areas. Vacuum your space as needed.
- Twice a month, use a long-handled duster to clean wood moldings, hanging light fixtures, and ceiling fans.
- Allow the changes of each of the seasons to be a reminder to perform exterior maintenance like cleaning out gutters and flower beds.
- Clean windows and sweep out exterior doorways as needed to free them from dust, spiderwebs, and any debris that may accumulate.

Since it must be done, find ways to make cleaning fun. Put on your favorite CD and crank up the volume. Lip-synch to your favorite tunes and hit the repeat button to replay that song that really gets your spirit moving. Involve your children in your cleaning routines. Remember, you are preparing them to create and care for their future sanctuaries.

Once you have cleaned the closets thoroughly, hang sachets for a pleasing effect. Place them in your dresser drawers, too. Cinnamon sticks and orange peels simmered in a pot of water on a stovetop is a very inexpensive way to scent your home. Use live rosemary topiaries or pots of lemon mint from a plant nursery or garden center to add a naturally sensational olfactory boost to your kitchen or dining room. Freshly cut flowers from your yard can be a delightful treat for any room in your home. These lingering scents remind you of the pleasure of having a clean home and serve as your offering to the Lord for providing your sacred space. They also provide low-cost aromatherapy every time you open the drawer or pass by the rosemary plant.

Cleanliness also shows respect for yourself, your family, and the space God has given you in which to live. Honor His gift by keeping your home clean and clutter-free.

STRENGTH

I thank you, Lord, for walls and floors
And ceilings nailed in place,
Because together they define
What is my sacred space.
Please give me strength to clean my home
When I am tired and weary
Remind me of my blessings, Lord,
When I can't see them clearly.
My work, the kids, my spouse, their needs,
They all depend on me.
I'd like to give my best to them,
But lack the energy.
The Bible says with You on board
That I can do all things,
Does that include the laundry loads
And the vacuuming?
Please help me, Lord, to do my best,
Without complaint or groan.
And help me use my gentle touch
To make this house a home.

Home Work

Look around. Is your home as clean and clutter-free as it could be? What are a few areas where you might begin to create a more blessed space?

_____

_____

_____

If your boss or your pastor were to drop by your home unannounced to visit you, could you comfortably invite them inside?

_____

_____

_____

If there was an emergency in the middle of the night, would you feel embarrassed if people had to come into your home to care for you or a family member?

_____

_____

_____

Select your days to power-clean and find ways to make cleaning fun for young family members. For example, see who can pick up their room the quickest or fill the toy box with one hand held behind their back. What other things can your family do to make cleaning more fun?

_____

_____

_____

Does your home reflect a commitment to comfort?

_____

_____

_____

What area of your home is your favorite spot for relaxation?

_____

_____

_____

Examine crucial areas of your home to ensure that they serve your family's needs first before considering how guests will use them.

1. *Lie on your child's bed to see how the mattress feels to your own back.*
2. *Add cushions to the wooden seats of dining chairs and stools to make meals more comfortable.*
3. *Take another look at your linens. Make sure that sheets, towels, and cloths are not threadbare. If so, replace them as soon as possible. If allergies are not a problem for your family, use fabric softeners to make your linens more comfortable.*
4. *Lightly spritz your pillow at night to encourage sweet dreams.*

5. *Appeal to your senses with a comfort food–scented candle to make your home feel cozier on a rainy or gray day. Try cinnamon spice, baked apple pie, and cookie scents.*

Consider hanging a mirror and a few pieces of artwork slightly lower than usual, perhaps at a school-aged child's level to help younger family members use and appreciate your home's furnishings, too.

A Prayer of Renewal

Heavenly Father, renew my strength and make me a good steward in my home. Touch my mind, my body, and my spirit and let caring for my home become a labor of love. When I am feeling overwhelmed, Lord, give me the wisdom to prioritize the things that must be done. And as I do my very best to make my home a special place, daily, I will rededicate it back to You. Amen.

Principle FIVE

Love People and Use Things

*Today, I will assure my family of their value
above any possession in our home.*

*My father used to play with my brother and me
in the yard. Mother would come out and say,
"You're tearing up the grass." "We're not raising
grass," Dad would reply, "we're raising boys."*
                                    HARMON KILLEBREW

*W*hen God blesses us to be able to furnish our homes
with things we love, we must be sure not to adopt a
haughty spirit. It is certainly okay to love our surroundings and make every effort to beautify our homes, but we
must keep things in perspective. We all know someone
who has a beautifully furnished room where no one is allowed or an expensive comforter on the bed where no one
sleeps. I visited many homes as a child where every surface in the house seemingly was covered in plastic. We
have to remember that no matter how expensive our *stuff*
is, it is still just stuff. Whether a lamp costs $500 or $5,
it is designed for the same purpose—to shine light into a
room.

Acknowledge that all *things* are replaceable. Sometimes we say and do hurtful things to people when they
mess with our stuff. Children usually never forget harsh
and angry words when they accidentally spill a glass of
juice on the rug or unintentionally break a treasured
plate. Years from now, you may have forgotten the inci-
dent, but the pain created by your harsh words may live
on in the heart of someone else for a lifetime.

King Nebuchadnezzar sure did love his stuff. His
home was a place of tremendous pride and joy. Considered

one of the Seven Wonders of the World, the hanging gardens of Babylon commissioned by King Nebuchadnezzar as a gift to his wife were magnificent even by today's standards. Chapter 4 in the book of Daniel tells us that Nebuchadnezzar would walk around his beautiful home and take credit for what God had allowed him to create. In Daniel 4:30 the king bragged saying, "Is this not great Babylon that *I* have built for the house of the kingdom by the might of *my* power, and for the honor of *my* majesty?" God was not pleased with the king's puffed-up attitude. The Bible goes on to say that immediately a voice from heaven declared, "The kingdom is departed from thee." King Nebuchadnezzar was driven away from all of the finery of his home and he was left in the likeness of a beast, eating grass from the fields. Verse 34 says that finally, when his understanding was restored to him, Nebuchadnezzar lifted his eyes to heaven and began to bless the Lord. This example might seem extreme, but it gives a clear depiction of how loving our stuff more than God and more than people can get us into serious trouble.

I have a real passion for collecting unique tableware, so much so that my family goes to auctions and estate sales to find it. My children quickly call my attention to any unusual plates, drinking glasses, or salt and pepper shakers that are up for grabs. On one of our forays, I spotted a beautiful set of hobnail goblets that I just had to have. After giving the winning bid, I packed up my prize and toted it home. I cleaned the goblets carefully and created a space for them in one of the built-in display niches in the breakfast room. My son, Braeden, who was five years old at the time, told me how proud he was that we were able to "win" the glasses with our bid. I was so excited about my acquisition that I decided to use my new goblets at the next Sunday's dinner. I carefully set the table for the four of us allowing Braeden to sip his beverage from one of my new glasses. He was careful to use both of his little hands to grip the goblet. After dinner, I began to clear the table and clean the dishes. Attempting to help, and without my knowledge, my son began to bring the remaining dishes into the kitchen. Suddenly, I heard a loud crash and the sound of breaking glass. Braeden let out a loud, "Oh no." I ran from the kitchen to see what had happened, and there he was, standing over the shards of broken glass. He was frozen in his tracks. When he looked up at me, he said in a weak, barely audible voice, "Mommy, I'm so sorry." I could see the tears welling up in his eyes and his confidence clearly shaken. I silently grabbed the broom and dustpan and began to sweep up the glass. Then I called his name.

"Braeden," I said as the tears began to roll down his cheeks. "Yes, I love those glasses, but they can't even compare to the love I have for you. You are far more important to me than they or anything in this house could ever be. It really is okay. Mommy is not upset with you." I bent over to kiss his little tear-stained face, when he wrapped his little arms around my neck as if he were hanging on for dear life.

"I love you, Mommy," was all he could muster after a few small sobs and a long sigh of relief.

Children are great barometers of how we assign value to our possessions. Such was the case with my friend Janice. When she and her husband, Hank, relocated to a new state and purchased a new home, they constantly reminded their five-year-old daughter, Danielle, to stay out of the living room. Janice was concerned that the white sofa, which so elegantly graced the room, would get soiled if Danielle played and climbed around on it.

Janice never gave much thought to the unspoken message she was sending to Danielle about the sofa and the living room and Janice's perceived value of those things. One evening when Janice and Hank were entertaining their new neighbors, the message, however, came out loud and clear.

As Janice greeted her guests at the door, she ushered them into the living room to be seated as Hank offered them hors d'oeuvres. She was astounded as she watched little Danielle run into the room and plead with the guests to come out of the living room immediately. "You can't sit there!" she said. "That's our 'for show' couch." Janice stood there, embarrassed, and turned several shades of red.

That poignant moment allowed Janice to hear the very message that she had been sending to her child. Unwittingly, she had assigned far too great a value to a possession instead of showing her daughter how to use, enjoy, and take care of the sofa. Many years later, Janice giggles when she retells the story of the incredible lesson that she learned from a zealous five-year-old.

We must be careful when we are raising small children that we do not set ourselves up to fail. Many new homes are designed with huge great rooms, replacing the traditional and separate living room and den. The great room should be furnished with children in mind, especially when they have no other indoor common spaces where they can play and relax. Consequently, white may not be the best color for such a space. Consider painting walls with washable paints. Slip-cover upholstered chairs in fabrics that either hide stains or can be tossed in the washer.

Tim and Maureen had the right idea when their children were young. These young missionaries traveled around the globe to foreign countries with three kids in tow, often living in tight, cramped quarters. When furnishing their many different homes, they made a decision to use sturdy, used furniture and hand-me-downs inherited from their families. Knowing that small children often climb and mark on the furniture, Maureen's "no hassle" approach made their environment comfortable and livable. Many years have passed and Maureen and Tim now live in an ivy-covered Tudor-style home, set in the middle of lush landscape and rose-filled arbors. Their children have grown older and their personal collections of home furnishings have also matured to antiques and fine furnishings, but the whole family's philosophy remains the same: "Love people and use things!"

Make your home livable. Value each other above all possessions. Keep the following in mind:

- Remember, antiques should be functional or used, displayed and appreciated. If you have items in your home of such great value that you must constantly guard against accidents or prefer that they not be touched, appropriately display them on high shelves or under lock and key, out of harm's way. No one living in or visiting your home should ever feel that your possessions are more valuable than they are.
- Treat your family as graciously as you would a visitor in your home. Weekly Sunday dinners, anniversaries, and birthday celebrations for them should be deemed "spe-

cial occasions" worthy of pulling out the good china, linens, and the silver service.

- Use adjectives such as "precious," "valuable," and "priceless" when describing loved ones, not possessions.

- Do not buy and prominently display toys for a young child if he or she is not allowed to play with them. To children, toys are meant for only one purpose, so allow children to enjoy toys and teach them how to take care of their things. The memories they will create by playing tirelessly with a favorite toy will far outweigh any monetary value that the toy may accumulate over the years. If you insist on buying toys as investments, buy two—one to play with and one to store in a safe place.

- Use your whole house.

- When space is tight, do not dedicate a whole room for an elaborate "guest room." Instead, give the space dual utility by replacing the bed with a comfortable sleeper sofa or beautiful daybed while using the room as a playroom, office, or hobby room.

- Use your home as a training ground to help your children prepare for their own future environments. Show them how to make good decisions about furnishings. Explain the choices that you make in using and supplying your home. Teach them how to properly use and care for your home and its contents. Allow children to have input as to how their rooms are filled and decorated.

Have faith!

- Having a beautifully decorated living room where no one is allowed to sit, carpet that no one is allowed to walk on, or a dining room suite where no one is allowed to eat is an absolute lack of faith. Subconsciously there is a belief that you will never again own anything quite as nice, so "that particular thing" must be preserved, even at the expense of someone's feelings.

- We often go to God when we desire a home and pray that He will grant us that desire of our hearts. Many times though, once God fulfills that desire, we forget all about Him and the promises and commitments we have made to Him. Remember, no earthly thing will last forever, so relax, don't take your stuff too seriously, and realize all of it is a blessing from the Lord.

Home Work

Do you have areas of your home that are just for "show" and are off-limits to yourself or your family? Why?

Does your family fear criticism if they do not do things exactly as you would do them? Ask! Talk to each family member, including your children, to see how they really view their home. Ask if they:

- *Feel that the home belongs to them too.*
- *Can feel comfortable in any part of the home.*
- *Feel that what they think and suggest about making the home more beautiful or comfortable really matters.*

Decide if you have subconsciously assigned a higher value to your possessions than you have to the people who are meant to enjoy them. Change the behavior immediately. Invite your husband to relax with you on the living room sofa. Pull out the special occasion dishes and eat from them at least twice a month. If one breaks, so what? Don't overreact. Instead, teach your children to properly use, respect, and care for the things that you love.

Principle SIX

Permeate Your Home with Spirituality

Today, I will make time to pray and meditate on God's Word in my home. I will treat my spiritual life as an element that is as essential to my well-being as the air that I breathe.

It is prayer that restores to us the ability to feel, to see and appreciate.

REUVEN HAMMER

*P*rayer was crucial in Job's house. He was continually in prayer for his children, offering up sacrifices for them daily. He sought the Lord on their behalf, asking God to cover their sins. Even more powerful was the strength of Job's prayer when he prayed for his friends. As we know from his story in the Bible, Job's faith and steadfast praying, even in the face of all possible disaster, saved his life and reversed his fortune.

Along my life's journey, I have had hopes and dreams to be and to do many things. The one thing, however, that remained a constant from my youth was my desire to marry and have children. What seemed like the simplest ambition was, at one time in my life, the most elusive.

I met my husband in college and fell deeply in love with him. After dating for several years, we married and began a wonderful life with new careers, a new home, and a newly kindled interest in building our personal relationships with God. We decided after two years of marriage that the time was right to start our family. We were both giddy with excitement at just the mention of the word *baby*. As a formality, I scheduled an appointment with my obstetrician/gynecologist to make sure that I would begin a pregnancy with a healthy body. During my routine exam, I noticed a look of concern in the doctor's face and a change in his tone as he spoke to the nurse. He instructed me to get dressed and come to his office where we could sit comfortably and talk. Having always been healthy, I was not overly concerned, but soon my face grew warm, my throat became dry, and my temples began to pound as I sat speechless trying to absorb the painful information he was delivering. The doctor calmly explained that clusters of fibroid tumors had invaded my body, but he assured me that the condition was common and operable. However, because of the unusually large size of my tumors, there was a great risk of sterilization after the surgery. I was devastated! My husband reassured me that he would accept and respect any decision I made about my own health and my own body.

After two surgeries, we tried unsuccessfully for two years to have a child. We used fertility medications and followed the doctor's dictates to no avail. The constant disappointments and false hopes began to take their toll on our marriage. It was increasingly difficult for my husband to come home and see me crying and distraught each month as my body confirmed that no child had been created within it.

One warm summer evening, my husband sat me on the bed and knelt beside me. He was so overwhelmed with emotion that he could barely fight back tears as he swallowed hard and began his difficult conversation. "Honey," he said, "I know this is hard. I also know that it is much harder for you than it is for me, but we have got to stop this. I can't bear to see you ride this emotional roller coaster any longer. I love you, and I want to spend the rest of my life with you—with or without a baby. We already are a family."

At that moment we decided to completely release this problem and cast our cares upon the Lord. We prayed together that night on our knees at our bedside and declared, "Lord, You know the desires of our hearts, but let Your will be done." As an act of faith, I immediately ceased using the prescribed fertility medications and I canceled another surgical procedure that the doctor thought could be beneficial. For the next few months we prayed together in our home, asking God for victory over this seemingly hopeless situation.

One crisp fall morning I was suffering from fatigue and flu-like symptoms and went to see my doctor, hoping he could prescribe medicine that could provide some relief. Before he would agree to medicate me, he insisted on a full examination and blood test. He had a clever smile on his face as he entered the examination room again. "Sorry, Mrs. Bailey," he said, "but I won't be prescribing any medicine today. We wouldn't want to do anything to harm your baby."

Like Job, I continually thank God for my family. In fact, I believe everything I have, including my home, belongs to God. Spirituality in the home environment is important for many reasons, so I take special care to treat our home as a sacred place.

Think about it. When we lay our heads on our pillows each night to sleep, all of our defenses are down. It is the time when we have the least control over our environments, and even over our very own thoughts. It is also a time when we must completely trust in God and believe that He will send His angels to encamp all around us to keep us safe during the night.

Through prayer and conversation with God, I invite

Him into my home daily to lead and guide my family and to make us loving toward one another. When serious disagreement, doubt, illness, or negativity arise, I walk through every room pleading the blood of Jesus. I pray with my children at home before a major test at school or with my husband before major decisions that may affect his or my career. When we have a special need or are seeking God for something specific, we gather the children together in one room with us to touch and agree as we seek God in prayer.

The Bible teaches us that there is power in the name of Jesus and at just the sound of that name demons tremble. Use this incredible power to keep negative thoughts, spirits, and attitudes away from your home and your family.

Before their departure out of Egypt, Moses instructed the Israelites to mark the doorways and posts of their homes with the blood of the sacrificial lamb so that when death consumed the first-born man and beast of all of Egypt, the Lord would see the sign of the blood and allow death to pass over the Israelites' houses. Today we do not have to take such measures, because we know that for those of us who believe, Jesus is the sacrificial lamb. Prayer and supplication in our homes mark our doorways.

Having the ability to speak freely the powerful name of Jesus throughout your home but choosing not to is like having a home equipped with electricity but never turning on the light switch. Turn on the power! Fill your home with spirituality and experience the joy and abundance the Lord has promised.

Janet had never before owned a home of her own. For

years she and her husband, Reggie, and their four children longed for their own home. The couple had racked up a mountain of medical bills when their youngest child was born with a myriad of birth defects. Their financial credit was in a dire state.

Over the years, they tried many things to overcome their financial woes. Both had worked second jobs, they cut back where they could, but still there never seemed to be enough money for a down payment on a home. Finally, a bankruptcy left them feeling like home ownership was a dream that would never be realized for their family. This hardworking couple, new in their relationship with God, had prayed in the past about their family's health challenges but had never asked God to intervene on their behalf concerning their financial challenges. They always had felt that, as responsible people, they should be able to handle their own money-related issues regardless of the circumstances and that somehow it was wrong to appeal to God for their natural needs.

Then one Sunday Janet and Reggie heard their pastor preach a sermon that changed their point of view. He told the story of Joshua, the son of Nun, and how the Lord had spoken to Joshua and promised him that if he remained strong and of good courage, God would give him and his people a victory while they were in pursuit of their promised home. The first chapter of the book of Joshua says that God promised to provide the land for them to enjoy if they remained faithful and obedient. Joshua then instructed the people to sanctify themselves and to expect a victory.

Before them stood the colossal walls of Jericho, an insurmountable obstacle. Before the people could fight this war and win the land, they had to have such a strong faith that they could shout the victory before the battle had even begun. They had to make such a confident, loud, and jubilant noise that it would destroy the wall—the very obstacle that stood between them and their promised place. Their praise was so great that it destroyed the wall of Jericho, bringing it flat to the ground so that God's people could walk right into the city.

The couple began to understand that because they had accepted Christ, they were joint heirs in the kingdom of God and all of the promises of God were theirs to inherit. Believing that God would make a way for them to obtain a home was ultimately not about the house but the act of faith in knowing that all things are possible with God.

Together, Janet and Reggie began to earnestly seek God for a home for their family. In 1 Peter 3:7 the Bible encourages husbands and wives to honor one another that they may be joint heirs together of the grace of life and that their prayers not be hindered.

Janet and Reggie set aside a day together each week to fast and pray collectively. They even requested their pastor to pray for God to respond to their need for a home. Then they began to thank God in advance for the blessed home He was going to provide for them.

One evening, while riding through their town in a residential area that had been rezoned and was being developed for commercial use, they saw a beautiful four-bedroom brick home. A man was pounding a sign into the front yard. They thought it was a for sale sign, so they pulled into the driveway of the home to inquire about the price. They assumed the gentleman was the real estate agent handling the sale of the property, but in fact, he was the owner of the home. He had an offer from a corporation to buy the land for a substantial amount of money to build a gas station on it. His agreement with them required that the land be cleared and ready for them to grade and begin to build on within four months. The home, which had not had an occupant for many years, needed some minor work but was in great condition. He hated to tear it down because it had been in his family for many years, but it had to be cleared away from the property. The gentleman did not want to incur the additional expense of having to do so. The house was not for sale, it was *free* to anyone who moved it off his land. Without a plan or much money, but lots of faith, Janet and Reggie agreed to take the house.

The next Sunday, Janet shared her testimony with her church about their blessing of the free house. Excited and energized by this miracle of God, their church family vowed to help them any way they could. One older deacon in the church, who owned many acres of land, donated one acre to the family.

Left only with the expense of moving the home, Janet and Reggie continued in faith as they began to prepare for their move. Their church family organized a fund-raiser for the family to help offset some of the expenses. They held a day in the park with games, contests, and great food, which was open to the community for a donation to the family's cause. A local reporter caught wind of the story and wrote a front-page article in the newspaper about the family. Within weeks, the community donated every penny the couple needed to move their new home to their new land.

Reap the benefits of a spiritual home.

- Designate a place in your home for daily prayer and meditation. Nearly eight hundred studies in the past ten years, including a recent Duke University study, confirm that people who have a consistent prayer life or meditate on a routine basis generally are healthier, heal more rapidly, and live longer, happier lives.
- Place a comfortable chair or an oversized floor pillow in a corner of a room where you can pray, read the Scriptures, quote positive affirmations, or just communicate with God.
- Create a prayer garden in your yard complete with bench and trickling fountain. Sit and enjoy it. Looking at beautiful flowers and listening to wild birds singing reminds us of the splendor of God.
- Surround yourself with books, tapes, and art that inspire and encourage you to be a more spiritual person. Keep these resources handy to help you transform negative thoughts and redirect your energy to create a positive outcome.
- Play music in your home that makes your spirit soar.
- Hang a decorative corkboard on which to attach inspiring quotes that you can read daily.

A special prayer for the home

Heavenly Father, thank You for Your grace and mercy and Your unwavering love. Thank You for providing food and shelter on this glorious day. God, strengthen the hearts, souls, and minds of all who reside here. Please send Your angels to protect this home as we sleep and slumber and order our steps from the moment we awaken each morning, until we return safely at the end of every day. Continue to keep Your loving arms around us as we strive to do what is pleasing in Your sight. Let this home be a place of peace and love. Keep strife and envy at bay. Let all who enter this home be blessed and when they leave it, allow them to carry with them a newly rekindled spirit of goodness and compassion. For with You as the source of our life, we build this house on solid rock, fortified with prayers and thanksgiving. Amen.

Home Work

Rent a tape or check out library books on meditation. Use a comfortable pillow to sit or kneel on while you meditate. Before permanently assigning an area of your home as your "sacred place," try out several different areas to see which is the most conducive for this type of contemplative activity.

If the practice of daily prayer or meditation is new to you, start slowly, beginning with five minutes and building up your time as it suits you. Record your innermost thoughts immediately after ending your meditative session.

List four words that describe how you feel after you have meditated or prayed.

_____

_____

_____

_____

_____

_____

Don't feel embarrassed or compelled to explain to family members your choice to pray or meditate if they do not understand or appreciate your need to grow spiritually. Do be honest and once you begin to feel the benefit of your spiritual exercises, share and lovingly encourage your family to participate.

Principle SEVEN

Consciously Set the Emotional Tone of Your Home

Today, I will decide to be a positive force in my home. I will make a conscious effort to create a loving environment, and I will not be so easily moved by the negative behavior of others.

Let the words of my mouth, the meditation of my heart, be acceptable in thy sight, Oh Lord.

PSALM 19:14

After having a disagreement with my husband and a restless night, I awoke the next morning in a miserable state. I scorched the grits, cooked the eggs too hard, and threw away the carton of sour milk I had accidentally left out on the counter all night. All this, before 9:00 a.m.!

When my children awoke, they did what they always do—jumped out of bed and greeted me with a big smile and hug. I gave each a quick squeeze and continued in my foul disposition. I noticed, after about an hour, the children's attitudes had changed. They, too, were scowling and complaining about everything. After another hour, they were arguing and running back and forth to me to tattle on one another. That's when it hit me! These children were feeding off my negative energy! I had set the tone of the temperament in the house, and they had unconsciously fallen into the same pattern. I knew right away I needed to change my actions and my thought process or I would ruin a precious day that God had given us.

I quickly gathered the kids and together we devised a plan of action. We would only do things today that would make us happy. After a trip to the library to pick out a collection of silly books like *The Adventures of Captain Underpants*, the three of us played outside on the swing set, pretending to race one another to the moon. After lunch and a nap, we pitched a tent in the living room, where we sang songs, ate popcorn, and drank orange juice chasers. The day was saved from my bad disposition.

I am now more aware of the power I possess in my family and in the world through my thoughts, my words, and my actions. Now I make a conscious effort to be sure those thoughts, words, and actions coincide with a positive, spiritual belief in a God-centered environment.

Apostle Paul encouraged Timothy in 1 Timothy 4:7 to exercise himself in godliness. This simply means to practice daily talking, walking, and laboring in love in the various environments in which he would find himself. Paul took great care in teaching Timothy how to treat people respectfully. We should learn to do the same, beginning in our own home. Remember, the feeling often follows the action. Here are some ways to consciously set the emotional tone in your home:

- Decide to act toward your family in a loving manner. Greet them with smiles, hugs, and kisses before you go your separate ways every morning and before you retire every evening.
- Be slow to anger, quick to forgive, and generous with praise.
- Refuse to be provoked into unseemly behavior in your home. If you would not yell or say unkind words in the presence of a visitor, refrain from those behaviors when no one else is looking. A behavior is either acceptable or not acceptable, period.
- Never allow your home to be held hostage to anger or to grudge harboring. Win battles with a spirit of loving kindness and forgiveness.

Set the example.

- Remember that the seed you plant determines the fruit you harvest. People who have warm and loving personalities are almost always sure to have children who share similar traits. The home environment is undoubtedly a tremendously influential factor in character development.
- Instead of bullying or nagging spouses and children into being who you think they should be, lead by example. Decide to give more of whatever it is you desire to receive from them. If you desire more love, give more love. If you want respect, be more respectful. Even if the payoff is not immediate, it is coming!
- Do not allow your children to say mean things and disparage one another. Physical fighting should never be permitted! Home should be the primary place where discretion and anger management are taught. There are many broken families where adult siblings do not speak to one another because parents allowed too many negative interactions in their childhood homes. Adults are obligated to provide positive leadership in the home.

Linda, her husband, Eugene, and their three daughters are a great example of setting the emotional tone principle. Linda has always been exciting, fun, and the more daring of the couple. Eugene, on the other hand, is mature, dependable, and conservative in his demeanor. This couple, who were married at a very young age, are a study in opposites, yet their love and respect for one another have allowed them to beat the odds and accomplish what many others like them have failed to do: maintain a loving home for more than thirty years. Each of their daughters is unique in her own way, but they share common bonds that have made them a tight-knit family.

Linda shared with me once that in all the years of raising her children, she had never once had an occasion to spank any of them. She and Eugene began to instill in their girls, seemingly from the womb, the importance of characteristics like respect of both self and others, trust, compassion, and honesty. The children naturally assimilated those values in a home that was filled with faith and values. Just as DNA from each parent melds with that of the other to create the physical traits of a child, parental attitudes and values in the home likewise meld to create the character of a child. Their simple yet effective approach to raising their daughters by their example of virtuous behavior has produced three accomplished young women: a physician, a successful undergraduate student, and an active, gifted, and talented high school student.

We must recognize that we cannot control the actions of others, but we can control how *we* interact and respond to others. We must be sure that we are not reserving all of our kindness and self-restraint for the office or for our church families. If we can spend a day at work without cursing at the boss or hours in church without lashing out at the pastor, then surely we can be equally charitable at home.

Queen Vashti's husband thought her to be an exquisite woman. He boasted about her beauty. He thought her grace and style surpassed any other woman in his or any other kingdom. But when they were entertaining guests in their home, Vashti had no time and little tolerance for her husband. When he sent a servant to ask the queen to come before him so that his guests could admire her, she embarrassed him by refusing to come. She felt that entertaining and pleasing her own friends was far more important than seeing that the king was satisfied. Queen Vashti's poor attitude and disregard for her family eventually caused her to lose her home.

Our attitudes and behavior deeply affect how comfortable we are in our homes. To paraphrase an old proverb: A man gets angry with his boss at work. He comes home and yells at his wife. The wife spanks the child who in turn kicks the dog. The dog chases the cat and heaven help the poor mouse who must face the wrath of that cat.

Understand the power of the spoken word. Choose to speak health, wealth, happiness, and power into your home. Words are so powerful they can build up or tear down your home and the people who reside in it. Death and life are indeed in the tongue. According to Proverbs 16:24, "Pleasant words are as a honeycomb, sweet to the soul and health to the bones." Likewise, Proverbs 15:18 says that an angry man stirs up conflict.

I grew up in a home where my father detested speaking of other people in a negative manner. He abhorred gossip and did not tolerate it in his home. He was diligent about keeping his children out of the presence of "talkers." He understood the power of words and how negative words breed hateful thoughts and actions. Such words are equally as harmful to the spirit of the speaker as they are to the spirit of the one who is being negatively spoken of.

Consider how you dialogue. Think about what you speak to yourself in your most intimate space. "I'm fat.

I'm broke. I can't. I do not have. I don't deserve. Nobody loves me." We have the ability to verbally torment ourselves. Our inner dialogue can be harsher than anything anyone could ever say to us. Instead, we should make our home a place where we build ourselves up. As the song says, we should accentuate the positive and eliminate the negative. Treat yourself at least as well as you treat others. Recognize that you set the tone for how others will treat you based upon how you treat yourself.

Use words to empower others in your home. Constantly encourage those who live there. This is crucial to creating a sanctuary. How we dialogue with our spouses is a choice. We can choose to criticize and verbally nitpick their every annoying habit or we can allow some things to be covered by love. "The soup is too hot, the juice is too cold. You can't handle money. You can never do anything right!" In your home, nasty words spewed like a venomous poison can kill love relationships. Once hurtful words depart from our lips, they cannot be retrieved. Ironically, it is usually at home where we feel free to denigrate others because we trust our loved ones to keep our dirty little secrets. No one will ever know, so we think, the destruction that we cause at home.

The Book of Proverbs has much to say about this. Proverbs 15:17 teaches us that it is better to dine on herbs in a house where there is love than to dine on meat in a home that is filled with hate. Proverbs, chapter 21, warns us that it is better to live in a small corner of the roof of a house alone than in a big house with a fighting woman, and better to live in the wilderness than in a house with an angry one.

Many times, I see homes in which only one spouse has

accepted and submitted himself or herself to God. Unfortunately, often when this happens, the born-again partner tends to take a superior attitude toward the spouse who has not yet come to Christ. They tend to throw their supposed "godliness" into the face of the unsaved partner. They say things like, "You just don't understand because you're not saved," or "We are just not on the same level spiritually." Know that your salvation is not something that you have earned or deserve. It is simply God's grace and mercy that brings us into a place of relationship and obedience to him. Do you think that God would be pleased being placed in the middle of such arrogant and mean-spirited conversation? In fact, 1 Peter 3:1 teaches us that if husbands do not obey the word, they may be won by the conversation of their wives. Likewise, chapter 3, verse 7, goes on to say that husbands should dwell with their wives according to knowledge giving honor unto the wife. Finally, this chapter of 1 Peter encourages spouses to be of one mind, having compassion for one another. It instructs us to be courteous and warns us not to do evil for evil. Refrain from speaking evil; look for and then proceed in peace. God's eyes are always on the righteous; that includes within the walls of our homes.

The words we choose to speak to our children in the privacy of our homes are so powerful they last a lifetime and often seep into future generations. Powerless and unable to defend themselves, our children often bear the brunt of all our problems, and home becomes a dreaded place of constant negative verbal bombardment. It is just as possible, even if it has not been your childhood home experience, to speak hope and success into their lives, instead of negative demeaning things.

When my son Braeden was about four and a half years of age, I made an exciting discovery. One evening when my husband Ray and I were putting away Braeden's laundry in his bedroom closet, I began to tell Ray a funny story about something that had happened to me earlier that day. My son, who had a quick wit and a robust laugh even at that young age, had been tucked into bed hours earlier. He was sound asleep, but every time I got to a really funny part of my story, even before my husband could respond, Braeden would let out a giggle. At first, we thought he was responding to his own dream, but as I continued on with the story, I realized that while his body was resting, his mind was still keenly aware of everything going on around him. He was laughing at my story.

I decided two things that evening. First, I would not allow him to fall asleep with the television still playing. Though we were extremely careful to monitor the shows that he watched, often sexually suggestive images and commercials were sandwiched between kid shows and early evening broadcasts. He could just as easily absorb from the television all of the negative imagery that we were attempting to shield him from.

Second, I decided to go into his room whenever possible while he was sleeping and to speak health, happiness, and godliness into his life. I whisper things to him like, "You are an awesome person. You are brilliant. God loves you and so do Daddy and I. You will grow up to become a leader and a very blessed man. Trust God." It is a practice that I continue until this day with both my son and daughter and, unbeknown to him, occasionally to my husband, too. It works!

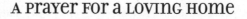

A Prayer For a Loving Home

Heavenly Father, please show me myself. Reveal in my spirit the places within me that are weak so that I may gain the strength necessary to be a vessel of honor in my home. Give me the desire, the courage, and the ability to grow in wisdom and in grace. Allow me to be more loving to You, Lord, to myself, and to my family. Help me to accept correction from You in the spirit of love with an open heart. Please help me to not let foolish pride keep me from saying, "I'm sorry," even when it isn't my fault. Lord, please don't let my words, my thoughts, or my actions be a source of pain or devastation to the spirit of others. Instead, God, allow me to use my hands, my head, and my heart to build up my house so that I may experience the fullness of Your splendor. Amen.

Home Work

Place a mirror at the entrance of your home that you use the most. Then, before leaving your house to go out into the world, face the mirror and speak something positive about yourself to yourself. Write five positive things you might say now.

_____

_____

_____

Say please and thank you to your children and insist they do the same with one another. Praise them often when they show acts of kindness to others. What are some habits your family might adopt to encourage kindness to each other? (Example: Say good night and God bless you before retiring each night, etc.)

_____

_____

_____

Challenge yourself. How long can you go without uttering a single negative word in your home? Seriously, try it! What are some of the negative responses you recall from your childhood?

_____

_____

_____

Principle EIGHT

Create an Atmosphere of Comfort and Joy

Today, I will carefully consider the emotional value of my home. I will use my home in ways that work best for my family and me.

Your heart shall rejoice and your joy shall no man taketh from you.

JOHN 16:22

I believe it is the will of the Lord that we have an abundance of both comfort and joy in our lives. Remember, even as Christ was preparing to leave His disciples He encouraged them, ensuring them, according to John 14:16, that "the Father shall give you another Comforter, that He may abide with you for ever."

He desires to be the center of our joy, and He wants us to share the essence of His joy with those with whom we interact on a daily basis. Our homes are an excellent place for us to bear witness to the comfort and joy of the Lord through our actions and our attitudes.

Contrary to the "taking it easy" notion that most people relate to the concept of comfort, the true meaning of the word *comfort* has a deeply spiritual connotation. *Merriam-Webster's Dictionary* defines comfort as "strengthening greatly" or "to give hope to." Designing a home with comfortable furnishings *is* essential to creating an enjoyable space, but when we seek to create a blessed home—a sanctuary, complete with comfort and joy—our primary focus should be on creating a positive and hopeful atmosphere.

We should strive to design an environment where our loved ones and we can feel secure, strengthened, and content. Never underestimate the importance of a positive atmosphere because within it God can produce miraculous results.

Take for example the story of Bartimaeus, the blind beggar whom Jesus and the disciples encountered as they journeyed together into Jericho. When the blind man cried out to Jesus, the Master commanded that Bartimaeus be brought forward. The first thing Bartimaeus was told to do by the disciples *before* he was to receive his healing was to be of good comfort. In other words, the disciples were telling the man to cheer up and be confident. By doing so, he was creating an atmosphere of faith, thereby providing the environment for Jesus to perform a miracle, restoring Bartimaeus's sight.

God performed a similar miracle of healing in William's life. William grew up in a home that provided him with little comfort. His parents were divorced when he was three years old and the legal battles left his mother bitter and angry. William inherited his father's stunningly good looks and charming personality, and not a day went by that William's mother did not remind him of that fact. Whenever young William made a mistake or did something that she thought was worthy of a lecture, she began her correction with, "You're just like your daddy."

His mother seemed to withhold real affection from him, afraid if she dared to love him freely, he would leave her too. William would overhear her talking on the telephone about his father, saying things like, "He ain't no good," or "All he knows how to do is chase a skirt." The negative messages and the "You're just like your daddy" retort played repeatedly in William's head throughout his childhood, making him believe that he, too, must be a no-good skirt chaser.

After college, William was finally able to afford his own apartment. His spirit still broken by his mother's harsh words, William began to live up to her expectations. He paraded beautiful women in and out of his home and his life until he was just tired of having so many women and yet never experiencing any real love.

During a Sunday worship service, William felt compelled to respond to an altar call. The minister asked who in the congregation was just tired of being outside of the will of God—tired of living a life that was spiritually unfulfilling, a life that felt meaningless.

That is exactly what William was feeling. He was tired of not having a deeper sense of purpose. He was tired of the many mornings he awakened to different women in his bed. He was tired of hearing his mother's cynical messages repeating themselves in his head. He sought God for forgiveness and for a healing of his mind and spirit, and God responded. William was then able to forgive. He forgave his father for choosing not to continue to love and care for his son the way a father should. He forgave his mother for her resentment and harmful words in his youth. Finally, he forgave himself for choosing to live in a manner that he knew to be unacceptable to God.

It was not long after William gave his life to Christ that he met the woman who is now his wife sitting in a pew across the aisle from him in a Wednesday night Bible study. Together they have created a new sacred space, consecrated by God, for themselves and their three sons.

One way to encourage comfort and joy in a home is simply to allow people to be themselves. The execution of this principle begins with you. You need to create a space where you feel your best. Decide what kind of atmosphere you have created. Is it a tense or pretentious environment or is it a calming, laid-back and kick-off-your-shoes kind of home? A blessed home is one where people gravitate to it because of the atmosphere, not the stuff that is in it.

When guests decide to spend time with you in your intimate space, it is their way of saying, "I want to enjoy you and I want you to enjoy me." I will admit, there were times when I chose to emphasize the appearance of perfection over the comfort of my loved ones. Oftentimes when my own family who live in another state would come to visit me, I would plan elaborate meals served up on my most beautiful hand-painted dishes. I would spend hours making sure that every aspect in the house was just right and heaven forbid some little detail was out of place.

When it was time to serve dinner, I was usually stuck in the kitchen, carrying platters back and forth while they sat and enjoyed each other. They would summon me in the dining room to join them or offer to help me in the kitchen so they could spend more time with me, but I would not hear of it. I would not allow *my* guests, even if they were my family, to have to lift a finger in my house. I now look back and realize how foolish I was.

On one occasion, my family arrived at my home while I was out scouring the grocery store for fresh herbs and spices to cook up my homemade spaghetti sauce. It would take additional time to cook the sauce once I arrived home. As the night fell, I encouraged them to wait a little while longer, and I promised them the best sauce they had ever tasted. Well, this hungry bunch could have cared less about my cuisine. One of them had enough prudence and gumption to order several large pizzas so that everyone could eat and go to bed after having traveled such a long way to visit me.

Another time, I asked one of my sisters to set the table for me so that we could enjoy our meal together. She obviously had had enough of me and my type A personality. She came prepared with her own arsenal. She had packed among her things a supply of paper plates and cups. I heard the muffled giggles coming from my dining room, but when I walked in with a platter of food, the whole room burst into rip-roaring laughter. "Okay, okay," I said, giggling too. "I give. If it is paper plates you want, then paper plates you shall have."

"It's not that we don't appreciate your efforts and everything you do to make us feel special, it is just that when we come to your house, we want you to relax and enjoy the time with us." Now we have our best conversations in the kitchen. Everyone is doing something to help prepare the meal, and I am not too exhausted or stressed to enjoy my guests.

One of the greatest blessings I have ever received concerning my home was during Thanksgiving several years ago. Some friends who settled in Charlotte from the Ivory Coast accepted our invitation to dine with us on this uniquely American holiday. I planned a meal that would adequately feed my family and this couple and their two young children. On the eve of Thanksgiving, I got a frantic call from my guests. They thought they were going to have to back out of dinner because some of their family and friends had unexpectedly shown up at their doorstep. They were hoping we could accommodate six extra people. "No problem," I said confidently. I had learned the lesson that comfort and joy have less to do with food and more to do with a loving attitude, which makes people feel accepted and wanted.

I supplemented my golden-roasted turkey, home-made cornbread stuffing, and Southern-style "sweet tea" with deli-prepared biscuits, potato salad, and apple pies. I spent my time greeting each of my guests with a sincere and heartfelt hug. We lingered for hours after our meal sharing stories from across two continents. For many of my guests, this experience was their first-ever Thanksgiving celebration and their first meal in the home of a native-born American.

It was music to my ears when I heard their children chime a chorus of "Aaahs" and "But we don't want to leave now." As my guests prepared to leave, one of the men who spoke French but very little English leaned and whispered to my friend who began to interpret the man's words.

In his native country, Zaire, it is tradition to pray and sing a blessing in a home where one has been treated with love and kindness. With our permission, he wanted to lead this musically gifted group in a song of blessings for my home. He began with a powerful prayer of thanksgiving, and in a low, sweet voice he led the group in a melodic song asking God to bless our home, our health, and our lives. This expression of love brought me to tears, and I will always cherish the memory of this touching experience.

Having joy in your home entails living in truth about yourself and your family. Just as the Prayer of Serenity declares, "Change the things that you can, accept the things that you cannot, and have the wisdom to know the difference." Seek God concerning the challenges in your home. It is not God's will that we live in constant worry and concern. Psalm 127:2 lets us know that it is pointless to get up early, sit up late, and be sorrowful because God gives His beloved sleep. To increase your level of comfort and joy in your environment, consider doing the following:

- Build or buy the best home that you can afford. Admittedly, home ownership may not be for everyone, but the advantages of owning, for most, outweigh any financial reason for not doing so.
- Choose to downsize in other areas of your life to make home ownership possible. Drive a less expensive car or eat out less. Spend less on designer label clothing.
- Live within or below your means so that financial stress does not rob your home's atmosphere of joy. If you cannot afford it, live without it.
- Never try to fit your home or your family into another family's mold. Concentrate on living the best life you can live within your own four walls. Spend more time getting to know who you are and what are your heart's desires. If you love being a city dweller and living in a fast-paced environment, you are very likely to be unhappy in a house in the country, miles away from the hustle and bustle with which you are accustomed.
- Finally, deal head-on with whatever challenges threaten your joy in your blessed space. We cannot afford to be naive in thinking that we are exempt from the cares of life because we are in Christ. Tragedy, strife, and hardships can touch any home; however, our faith in God brings us comfort even in our times of crisis. For those who believe, in spite of occasional moments of uncertainty and instability, we can still experience comfort and joy. The Bible tells us in Psalm 30:5, "Weeping may endure for a night, but joy comes in the morning."

A Prayer of Restoration

Heavenly Father, I repent back to You for not always choosing to live well and to the best of my ability. Like the Prodigal Son, there were times when I have lived beneath my privileges, choosing to eat from the trough of the swine rather than from the table of my father, the King. For this, Lord, I ask Your forgiveness for You have not authorized my needless sufferings. I know, according to Your Word, that through the power of the Holy Ghost, You will fill my heart and my home with comfort and joy. Restore me and my household and I will continue to seek Your face for Your guidance and Your wisdom so that all who grace my doorstep will feel Your presence. Let Your love radiate in the atmosphere and Your name will be glorified in my life and my home. In Jesus' name, Amen.

Home Work

Have you used each room in your home to best suit your needs or have you limited yourself to only using your spaces in ways for which they are originally designated? Think of a room you'd like to change and list a few ways you could do so to make it more comfortable or enjoyable.

_____

_____

Are you realistic about your expectations, considering how you live and how you have chosen to beautify your home? Explore how you can improve and adjust the way you choose to live in your sacred space so that it will be pleasing to God.

_____

_____

Do you constantly compare your family or your home and its furnishings to that of friends and neighbors? If so, how? Be honest in your answers.

_____

_____

Concentrate on what makes your situation special and rejoice in that. Make a list of things about your family and your home that are unique. Think of ways to strengthen and encourage them.

_____

_____

Principle NINE

Use Your Home as a Place to Relax and Rejuvenate

*Today, I will examine the most demanding
commitments in my life both in and outside the home
and recoup some of my valuable time and energy
for my family and myself.*

Allow yourself to do something you enjoy, even if no one else cares to join you. Make your own fun. Pamper yourself. Use playing and puttering to rejuvenate your energy.

ANNIE TYSON JETT

*C*ountless people run through their lives at breakneck speed without taking any time to enjoy daily experiences and indulgences. In our society we have been fed a steady diet of "you can have it all and you can do it all, right now!" Our children are so deeply involved in a plethora of extracurricular activities that they show signs of stress, depression, and fatigue that were never seen in past generations. The minivan has replaced the dinner table as the place for families to eat, make plans, and have intimate conversations. For many, home has become the place to get a fresh change of clothes, a quick shower, a microwaved meal, and a minimal amount of sleep.

Even in my own life, I have too often put relaxation and rejuvenation on the back burner while I attempted to fill the roles I thought my family expected of me. By day, I was a stay-at-home mom and an entrepreneur with a demanding new business. By night, I worked outside of the home. I was deeply involved in my community, my son's school, and my church, leaving only four or five hours in my day for sleep. I was exhausted! While I was doing what I thought was best for my family, I was riddled with guilt because I knew that no one was getting to enjoy the very best of me, the essence of who I really am. When my budget allowed me to purchase a new outfit for myself, I somehow always managed to buy something for the children instead. I was meticulous about grooming my children, and yet months went by between manicures and hair salon appointments for me. I was no longer the fun-loving, witty, caring person that I had always been. I was just tired!

My lack of play and pampering began to take its toll. At my husband's insistence, I went to see a doctor about my low energy level, headaches, and inexplicable body aches and pains. As the doctor began a complete physical examination, he asked me questions about my lifestyle. The diagnosis, it seems, was one that was becoming all too common. I, like many of his patients, was suffering from burnout. Fortunately, the exam showed no physical problems. The doctor assured me, however, that continued stress and lack of rest would eventually manifest as illness in my body. He insisted that I make some changes immediately! He told me that if I was unhappy and tired, I certainly could not make my family happy. To change this unhealthy pattern I first had to honestly ask myself what I had hoped to gain from such personal martyrdom. The answer: I wanted my children to see me as hard-working and intelligent. I wanted my husband to feel as if I were making equally important contributions to our family. Realistically, these are things that they had undoubtedly felt about me all along. I *really* was trying to prove my worth to myself.

I mustered the courage to quit the evening job and restructure my business, taking on a partner to help shoulder the responsibilities. I began to say no to requests that would deplete my energy and time. Now, on occasion, I splurge on a small luxury for myself. A new hairdo makes me feel confident and a new fragrance makes me feel alluring. A thirty-minute jog or a midnight bubble bath renews my energy and allows me to think without interruption. My entire family benefits when I take greater care of me. I accept that I am valuable to my family just because of who I am, not just for the things I do for them. Give yourself permission to rest.

After spending six days designing all of creation, even God took a day of rest. Yet, we find it so difficult to allow ourselves time to relax and rejuvenate. It is not some haphazard coincidence that the God Who made all of heaven and earth would want us to know how important resting really is. We are, after all, made in His image. Just know that the creature is never wiser than the creator. If the all-powerful God opts to rest, perhaps we should, too.

Once, after delivering an hour-long motivational speech for a mother's support organization, I began fielding questions from this astute group of women. When the session concluded, I grabbed my coat and purse and headed toward the door, when a petite hand nervously touched my shoulder. "If I could just ask you one more question," this mom said. "How can I not feel guilty about wanting downtime at home away from my husband and children?" Even among her peers, who all at some point in time had probably shared the same sentiment, she was uncomfortable openly confessing her need for rest and private time at home. I told her that I found her question refreshingly honest.

I shared the following with her: When I was at one of the most difficult times in my life I recognized the damage that not taking time for me could do to my relationships at home. I was burning the candle at both ends and in the middle. I was grouchy and short-tempered. One day, my daughter came bouncing into the living room where I sat reading a book. "Mommy," she said. "Can you go outside with us to play soccer?" My son, recognizing the exhausted look permanently fixed on my face, tried to console her and said, "That's okay, Brinn. We can wait until Daddy gets home. He's the fun one." Boy did that hurt!

Daddy, it seemed, was willing to spend more "fun" time with the kids. He was creative in finding ways to play with them and get rest too. When he needed a quick nap, he tussled with them, tired them out, and then played the "quiet game." The children would close their eyes and try to trick Dad into thinking that they were asleep. Wouldn't you know it, without fail, they always ended up really falling asleep, leaving him free to grab some nap time for himself so that he could be rejuvenated when they awoke.

We all need to remember that rest and rejuvenation are of primary importance in any home. Learn to prioritize your time and energy, ensuring that you and your family are at the very top of the list. Understand and acknowledge that careers, school, and other commitments are demanding and can monopolize your time and drain your energy, leaving you with very little of either to really enjoy your most intimate space with the people you love.

Create some "down" time at home. You are not obligated to be "on call" for the whole world all of the time.

- Unplug all outside communication, figuratively and literally, for at least one hour every day. Use that time for uninterrupted dinner conversation, or gain cuddle time on the sofa with your spouse, your kids, or even your pet.
- Sleep late on an occasional Saturday. Have or serve breakfast in bed for no special reason instead of saving such an indulgence for times when you or your loved ones are ill. Never underestimate the power of purposeful play and relaxation to make your home life more interesting and cohesive.

Invest in:

- A luxurious bathrobe
- Wonderfully scented bath and massage products
- A feather bed
- A tabletop relaxation fountain
- A soft chenille throw
- Lots of comfortable pillows
- Plush towels
- High-thread-count bedsheets
- Incredibly comfortable slippers
- A lightly scented linen and laundry spray

Romance your home.

- It does not matter whether you are deeply in love or quite content alone, bring romance into your home. Fill your bedroom with fragrance from a deliciously scented candle, a bowl of potpourri, or the aroma of fresh-cut flowers. Love yourself!

- Designate a television-free zone where you can have complete stillness and quiet. It need not be a huge space, but the corner of a room equipped with a comfortable chaise or an overstuffed chair and ottoman will work fine.
- Use candlelight and miniature lamps to make your home feel cozy and special while hiding a room's flaws that are more apparent with harsh overhead lighting. Invest in dimmer switches to easily control the intensity of home lighting and create different moods and effects.

Nourish yourself: mind, body, and spirit.

- Exercise regularly. Take a class and learn something new like yoga, cooking, self-defense, or art. Such classes may help you relax and give you skills that you can incorporate into your life at home.
- Use your home as a place to pamper yourself and your family. It is a place to re-energize and re-focus. Put as much effort into taking care of yourself as you do in taking care of your children or spouse. By doing this you will have your "best self" to share with your family.

At the beginning of every spring, amid a landscape of blooming tulips, daffodils, and grape hyacinths, Dianne and her friends gather in her garden for their annual Divas Spring Fling party. Each event is a celebration of their friendship as much as it is an observance of their shared love of gardening, pampering, and great food. The entire afternoon is filled with activities for these six special friends. An exercise instructor is recruited to kick off the festivities with a lively routine that each of the ladies eagerly learn and commit to memory to incorporate into their daily exercise regimens. A masseuse sets up her table under the rose arbor where she will knead and crack tightened backs and stiffened necks. The patio holds the temporary manicurist station where fingers and toes are pampered to perfection.

Dianne's guests don breezy sundresses and wide-brimmed hats while they eat a wonderful catered lunch featuring dishes concocted with fresh herbs from a nearby farm. Afterward, the ladies sit lazily by the pool sipping herbal tea and enjoying the sounds of the bubbling fountain nearby, dreaming about next year's Spring Fling.

What Dianne and her friends have learned is how to take care of themselves, celebrate their friendship, and create a sanctuary each year in her backyard. Consider incorporating a day of rest each week into your family's routine. Teach the children to respect that day as "Family Day," when they cannot make plans with friends or try to catch up on homework alone in their rooms. Plan family activities together; even reading quietly in the same room can be a part of the day. Whatever you decide to do, keep the day sacred. Make time to express gratitude, become centered, and rejuvenate your connection as a family.

Home Work

Prioritize! Make a list, in order of importance, of the activities in your life that you must give time and attention to. Then carefully examine your activities each day for one week to see if you are wisely using your time in areas of your life that you deem to be of great value to you.

HOW I SEE MY PRIORITIES IN
THE ORDER OF THEIR VALUE
TO MY LIFE (LIST THE MOST
TIME-CONSUMING FIRST)

HOW I ACTUALLY SPEND
MY TIME ON THE THINGS
THAT I VALUE THE MOST

1._____   1._____

2._____   2._____

3._____   3._____

4._____   4._____

5._____   5._____

List four activities that you could do at home to indulge someone that you love dearly.

_____

_____

_____

_____

Now do those four things for you!

List four family activities that will strengthen your commitment to each other, promote personal growth, and stress the importance of spirituality on a weekly basis.

_____

_____

_____

_____

Principle TEN

Personalize Your Space

*Today, I will find ways to make my home unique.
I will incorporate my family's interests and
personality into our home.*

Have nothing in your home that you do not know to be useful or believe to be beautiful.

WILLIAM MORRIS

*K*ing Solomon lived among the things he loved. After he built the Lord's house, he built one for himself. He constructed a throne of ivory and gold. The six steps leading to the throne were lined with twelve lions, one on each side of each step. There was no other throne room in any kingdom that could compare to Solomon's. How regal he must have felt sitting in the midst of such beauty and magnificence. Though we may not possess the wealth of Solomon, we can learn from his example by having things in our homes that provide a sense of pleasure.

Ray has a nutcracker toy soldier that stood guard under his family's Christmas tree in their tiny apartment where he grew up. It has traveled with us through every move of our married lives and has found refuge in our current home, too. Ray is a quiet and introspective man who expresses very little attachment to possessions. It puzzled me that he insisted on keeping and displaying this ragged soldier over the years.

Needless to say, I made many attempts to convince him to throw it away. I even offered to buy him a brand-new one with shiny new buttons on the jacket that could stand proudly upright to guard our children's gifts at Christmas, but he flatly refused! Then, one chilly Christmas Eve as we sat together in our garage, sipping cocoa and assembling the last of the

children's toys, he finally shared with me the significance of the toy soldier.

He had grown up in a home without much overt expression of joy. Christmastime, however, was different. It
was a time of excitement and anticipation, and his
family's mood was lighter and happier. There was constant pie baking and biscuit making. Friends and family
came by and lingered in the kitchen while his "mama,"
Mary, whipped up something delectable to the sound of
the O'Jays crooning Christmas carols on the radio. So,
while I had only seen a ragged, dog-eared toy, to Ray, the
soldier represented some of the happiest times of his
young life. Now I cherish the idea that something so
simple and small can evoke such memories of joy.

Use cherished family heirlooms or favorite items from
your childhood to decorate your home.

• Enjoy the process of designing your home. A great
  home is one that has evolved over time.
• Be flexible. As you and your family mature and change,
  so will your needs and tastes.
• Collect and tastefully display the things that you love
  and are passionate about.
• Choose not to allow the negative unsolicited opinions
  of others who do not share your space to influence your
  tastes.

Camille has always loved doll babies. She began to collect them after her parents presented her with her first
porcelain one on her seventh birthday. Over the years, she
has collected dolls in almost every conceivable color and
theme. They have moved with her from house to house,

and she proudly and tastefully integrates them in nearly every room of her home. She has made great friends with a group of local ladies who, like Camille, collect dolls with a passion. She often hosts teas for her group, and they have even created a charity to find, repair, and donate dolls to Alzheimer's patients. Sometimes visitors disapprovingly comment on the number of dolls she has collected, and some have even taken the liberty of suggesting that she get rid of them. They have insinuated that the dolls intimate a streak of immaturity in her character. Those people, however, rarely get invited back to Camille's home. She feels strongly that she has a right to quietly enjoy her living space and its decor without having to please people who have no stake in her personal space. While it is important to have a charitable home, as we'll read in Principle Eleven, it is equally important not to allow others' negative opinions to invade the emotional tone of your home.

Take time to know and develop your own taste and sense of style.

- Find unique ways to incorporate special or inherited pieces into your decor that suit your specific needs. Turn an antique sideboard into a bathroom vanity or top a farmhouse table with marble and use it as a kitchen island. An oversized heirloom bed can find a new life as an ornate bench with the help of a wood craftsman.
- Have a special quilt designed to chronicle your family's life. Use fabric scraps from clothes that hold special memories, such as a graduation gown, the first tutu, or a Little League football jersey.

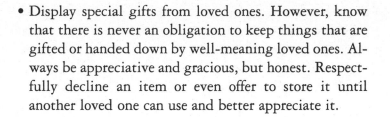
- Display special gifts from loved ones. However, know that there is never an obligation to keep things that are gifted or handed down by well-meaning loved ones. Always be appreciative and gracious, but honest. Respectfully decline an item or even offer to store it until another loved one can use and better appreciate it.

Entering the home of my artist friend, Luis, is an experience of sheer delight. A first-generation American born to Portuguese parents, art is in his blood. Both his parents are painters and sculptors, so when Luis began to show signs of his extraordinary talent at the early age of four, no one was surprised. Unlike most families, when he and his siblings drew on the walls of their bedrooms, his parents didn't complain; in fact, they encouraged it! Luis's use of vivid colors and exaggerated, abstract shapes have garnered him numerous awards and honors. He, however, considers the home that he shares with his wife and daughter to be his finest work of art. His wife, Naomi, and daughter, Marta, are artists, too.

Together, they've painted their home's interior walls in bright, bold colors reminiscent of flowers growing wild on the hillsides of Luis's parents' South American home. The brilliant colors make the perfect backdrop to Luis and Marta's contemporary paintings that line the walls in gallery juxtaposition. No room goes untouched; even the bathrooms are treated to luscious murals created by this family. Naomi finds practical uses in their home for the beautifully designed pottery pieces she creates.

This colorful home may seem overly stimulating to some, but it has just the opposite effect on Luis's family.

Their home stirs up feelings of passion, freedom, and self-expression. They are constantly surrounded by art that they have created with their own hands and imaginations, and in the eyes of this family, their home is indeed a masterpiece!

Select a decor that speaks to who you really are.

- Consider your home's interior style and decor to be a direct reflection of the people who reside there. Select colors, furniture, art, and fabrics that speak to who you really are. Look around your home and take cues from things that you have already acquired. Chances are, a predominant color or theme will surface.
- Be confident about your choices.

Use color to your advantage.

- Be creative. Research shows that colors have a significant effect on our moods and attitudes. If a familiar color from a childhood home makes you feel secure or happy, incorporate it into your decor. If bright colors make you feel stimulated, relegate their use to areas where you need to be focused and attentive. Avoid using them in bedrooms or other areas of the home you may use to relax and unwind.

Allow your passions, hobbies, and collections to tell something about you.

- Look objectively at your interior rooms. Anyone visiting your home should be able to sense something about your family's interests and personality in a matter of minutes upon entering it.

- Be innovative. Feel free to use unlikely items for decorative purposes. Make color copies of baseball trading cards and use them to decoupage a wood-framed mirror for the room of a sports enthusiast. Hang your child's first violin or create a still life of a collection of string instruments as art. Turn a favorite pair of cowboy boots into lamps for a western-themed room.

Put your heritage on display.

- Scatter photographs of several generations of family throughout the home or display collectively to form a gallery effect.

You don't need to be an artist to be creative. Photocopy old and recent black-and-white family photos onto iron-on transfer sheets purchased from an office supply or craft store. Buy or make a pillow using inexpensive light colored cotton duck or linen. Iron the transfer onto the fabric before stuffing the pillow and create a one-of-a-kind pillow that celebrates your family's lineage.

- Display mementos from your ancestral homeland on bookshelves or prop up items on decorative display shelves. Native fabrics can be made into pillows or throws.

Patrice and Bill did most of the restoration in their 1800s Georgian-style home themselves. Even though she is not a formally trained decorator, every room of their home could easily rival the fine rooms of a designer show house. They have infused their home with sparkle and personality. From the bead-board ceiling and crisp white wainscoting in the hardworking mudroom to the cotton candy–painted effect in their daughter's room, no space in the house evades Patrice's attention.

She has relied on her crafty discount shopping skills to acquire one-of-a-kind chandeliers and equally unique antiques for their home. Faux paint techniques transform a dwelling, which could have been overly formal and stoic, into an elegant yet comfortable home that doesn't take itself too seriously. Over the years, Patrice's family and friends have admired her work and have attempted to persuade her to design homes professionally. Ironically, she has no interest in pursuing financial gain for her talents. She simply says that it is a love for her family, not money, that motivates her and brings out the very best of her decorating talents.

Home Work

Think about the things that you have acquired in your home that are special to you. List them and explain why they are special to you.

_____

_____

_____

Which of your favorite things are stored away or go unused for months at a time? Rediscover them and remind yourself what special ties bind you to the item. Then, get creative and find a new use for the item that will allow you to see or use it on a regular basis.

_____

_____

_____

Identify any item you may have in your home that you neither like nor use any longer. Find someone who would use and appreciate that item, then give it away.

_____

_____

_____

Pretend to be a first-time visitor to your home. Look around, and list three things a visitor could easily tell about you or your family's interests.

_____

_____

_____

_____

What are your favorite colors? How do they make you feel? How can you incorporate them into your decorating scheme? Remember, if you are still afraid to make permanent changes, use colorful dishes, pictures, and linens to put your favorite colors into your home.

_____

_____

_____

_____

What one-of-a-kind memento can you create for your home? For example, create place mats using your children's drawings or doodlings of your own. Make four-color copies on a laser printer at a self-service copy shop. Have each picture laminated and use them as unique place mats.

_____

_____

_____

_____

Principle ELEVEN

Have a Charitable Home

Today, I will create a charitable home. I will encourage my family to share what we have, what we have outgrown, or what we no longer need. I will be humble in my charitable giving.

The liberal soul shall be made fat: and he that watereth shall be watered also himself.

PROVERBS 11:25

*K*ing Solomon, the son of David, was abundantly blessed where he lived. Like his father before him, he was faithful to God. Because Solomon's only request of the Lord was to rule over the people of God justly and with great wisdom, God was pleased. He bestowed upon Solomon's house not only material wealth but a reputation so greatly admired that it astounded other nations.

The queen of Sheba heard of Solomon's great name and of the beauty of his home. So great were the tales of his fame that she did not believe them. She traveled to his home to see for herself if the stories that had reached her homeland had merit. The queen was impressed beyond her wildest expectations.

Everything in Solomon's house exuded the same spirit of excellence that had caused him to please the Lord. His home was a sanctuary—special, consecrated, and like no other she had ever seen. The queen of Sheba observed the meat of his table, his servants, and his ministers. She was awed by the fineness of their clothing. She confessed to the king that she had not believed the reports of his wisdom and prosperity until she had been able to witness it with her own eyes. But most remarkable to the queen was the level of happiness in Solomon's home.

He was kind and generous with the people who lived

in his home and throughout his kingdom, and they were happy. 1 Kings 10:8 says that his men were happy. His servants were happy. They were delighted just to be in his presence, to stand before him and hear his wisdom.

She was so overwhelmed by the king's justice, the queen of Sheba was moved to gift him with even more riches, as did every man who journeyed to Solomon's home to seek the wisdom that God had put upon his heart.

Quick thinking and a desire to use her home to bring comfort to others marked a very special episode in Terri's loving relationship with her grandmother. Mildred, her maternal grandmother, had always been her favorite "nana." The elderly woman, an avid gardener, came to Terri's home every spring to guide her in planting and pruning the antique roses that she had given to her granddaughter many years before. The two ladies enjoyed this ritual for several decades.

One spring, while giving the plants an evening watering, Mildred's leg became entangled in the garden hose, and she slipped and fell, severely bruising her hip. Terri insisted that Mildred stay on with her while she recovered from her injury. The only problem, she decided, was that it would be too difficult for her eighty-year-old grandmother to climb the stairs in her historic Victorian home to reach the suite of bedrooms. Remembering how much Mildred enjoyed the garden, Terri was inspired with the perfect solution. She removed all of the furniture from her grand dining room, which had a glorious view of the gardens, and converted it into a makeshift bedroom for Mildred. Mildred could watch Terri garden and instruct her through the open French doors in the dining room, while enjoying the roses as a gentle spring breeze continually blew their fragrance indoors.

Many years later, when Mildred had passed away, Terri began to read the journals her grandmother had kept faithfully for nearly sixty years. As she pored through the volumes of memories, Terri was deeply moved that her grandmother had recorded their times together each spring with such love. She had listed the spring of her injury and her stay in Terri's dining room as one of the best visits and most memorable times with her granddaughter. What had meant the most to Mildred was Terri's willingness to change the order of her home to create a place of comfort and convenience all for her sake. A truly blessed home is one where people and their needs take precedent.

What is charity? The common perception is to give away something that you have to someone who is poor. This definition can be encompassed in the concept of charity, but the Bible clearly defines charity as love. 1 Corinthians 13 says that even if we speak the language of men and of angels but we do not have charity, or pure love, we are as sounding brass or a tinkling cymbal. In other words, a lot of noise and little substance.

All acts of kindness that are a result of your love for God and others fall under the auspices of charity. The spirit in which the gift is given is as important, if not more so, than the gift itself. There are three components to consider when you are creating an atmosphere of charity in your home. The first component is faith. Sometimes God will whisper into our spirits, or as some choose to say, lay it on our hearts, to give away something that is of value to us without the knowledge of how it will be replaced. This kind of charity is one that requires total faith and confidence in God.

Remember the starving widow and her son in 1 Kings 17 who were preparing their last portion of oil and meal as they readied themselves to die because of the famine in the land? God told his servant Elijah the Tishbite that He had spoken into the spirit of a widow woman a command to feed him. When Elijah journeyed to the city of Zarephath, he found the woman and the son preparing their last meal before death consumed them. Elijah asked the woman for a piece of her bread. This poor woman declared to him that she didn't even have a loaf of bread, just a handful of meal and a little oil, enough for her and her son. Then Elijah did something that many would think unconscionable. He asked this poor woman to feed him first. The widow was obedient to the servant of God, believing nothing but the Word of the Lord as it was revealed through Elijah, so she fed Elijah first. As he promised, they were continuously fed throughout the famine. The Bible says that every time the widow woman went to her barrel to get more oil and meal it was miraculously replenished. God made sure that her charity was not forgotten by giving her an endless supply to meet her needs. What faith it must have taken to give up something that was so precious and so badly needed by the giver.

The second component is humility. This element of charitable giving is one I witnessed my parents live by throughout my life. My now deceased father, Lawrence, was a grocer by profession, but he often painted houses and performed minor home repairs for elderly people in our community who could not otherwise afford those repairs. In exchange, he often received only a few dollars and perhaps a cake or a pie as payment. He always extended credit to families who already had overdue bills or perhaps not the best history of payment because he knew that they had children who needed to eat. His constant refrain to us children was, "Don't judge other people, because you are more blessed than you will ever know." What he was attempting to instill in us was that everything he had managed to obtain for his family was with the help of God. Though he worked hard to take care of us, it was God's grace and mercy that made so many things possible in our blessed home. He trained us to never mention the things we gave away to other people. He warned us about the embarrassment and hurt we could inflict upon others by openly recognizing the shirt or shoes we had once worn that now clothed another child. Real charity edifies or builds up the person on whom you are bestowing the act of kindness and love. We knew our dad would never receive credit or praise for many of his gifts of charity. But then his charity was never driven by reward and recognition. The Bible teaches us that when we give to be seen by men, we receive our reward in *their* praise, but when we do things privately, a greater reward awaits us in heaven.

The final component of charity is selflessness. So often when the church or a civic group organizes a clothing drive for the needy, we reach in the very back of our closets and pull out our 1970s jumpsuits and platform shoes. We give to charity all the junk we can't manage to sell at our yard sales. That kind of charity is easy, but can we give away that suit in our closet with the price tag still dangling from it? Can you give of your time when you are busy and it is most inconvenient for you?

My mother, Eunice, continues to live by the principle of having a charitable home. She has always been willing to share whatever she has—food, money, or time—even with perfect strangers. As a child, I remember her buying extra winter socks, hats, and scarves and then giving them to children in our neighborhood who did not have them. When a fire destroyed the home of a relative, my mother offered our home as a temporary refuge for their family, and she offered it again to another relative under the same circumstances. Mom continues to take in or take care of relatives who are ill or recovering from illness. A beloved cousin, Henrietta, who recently succumbed to cancer, called my mother her "angel" because she always appeared when she needed her the most. In all her giving, Eunice never asks for anything in return, and although she genuinely loves people, she continues to extend herself so unselfishly because, as she simply puts it, "I am doing all that I know to please God."

In order to have a charitable home, and be a charitable person, you must learn to give from the heart.

- Remember, as your giving increases, so do your blessings.
- Don't make the mistake of being so attached to possessions that you cannot give up something to someone in need.
- Work diligently to make a difference in the lives of others. Make this a family affair. Home is the first place where children should learn to be charitable and kind.
- Whenever possible, give anonymously without seeking recognition or reward for your kindness and generosity.

Rid your home of clutter to open your home and yourself to receive.

• Clean out cabinets, closets, attics, and basements at least once a year and donate unused or unwanted items to your favorite charity. Don't just give away the junk! If something isn't in good repair, throw it away; don't give it to someone less fortunate.

Develop a discerning spirit.

• Be aware that giving is a blessed act, but we must be careful that we are not taken advantage of by those who blatantly misuse the people of God for their own gain. There are con artists who travel from city to city preying on the generosity of godly people. Some even claim to be sent by God to get something from you. Be wise—wise as a serpent, the Bible says. Even in the story of Elijah and the widow woman, God had forewarned the woman that He was sending His prophet to her home. The words that Elijah spoke were a confirmation for what God had already told her.

Home Work

List several charities or causes that are special to you and why.

_____

_____

_____

_____

Explain to other family members why it is important to give and share your time and talents with others who are in need or less fortunate. List several ways your family can help those less fortunate. Here are a few ideas to get you started:

- *Start a "family do" jar of small tasks that your family can do to help an elderly or disabled neighbor.*
- *Have the entire family help bake cookies to sell to family and friends, and give the proceeds to the humane society or other charity of your choice.*
- *Organize a community yard sale and give the proceeds to a worthy cause, or collect blankets and distribute them at the homeless shelter.*
- *Allow children to donate toys that they have outgrown between birthdays and holidays. Allow them to personally deliver them to Goodwill or a battered women's shelter.*

_____

_____

_____

_____

Principle TWELVE

Build on a Foundation of Integrity

Today, I will choose to live in truth and integrity in my home.

The just man walketh in his integrity: his children are blessed after him.

PROVERBS 20:7

*R*elationship and financial integrity are paramount in creating a sanctuary. Understand that living in dishonesty of any kind in your home will slowly eat away at the very fabric that is designed to keep a home intact. Dishonesty can completely destroy relationships and make home a very undesirable place to be.

Queen Esther's integrity was tested in her home. As so charged by her cousin, Mordecai, she kept a part of herself, the fact that she was of Jewish descent, hidden away from her husband, King Ahasuerus. There came a point when Haman, a high official in King Ahasuerus's empire, conspired to have Mordecai and all of the Jews in the kingdom killed. Esther was grieved at the news of Haman's plan, but she feared more for her own life and was hesitant to reveal her people's plight to the king. Mordecai sent her word that if she chose to hold her peace, she too would be destroyed along with her father's house. The king's quarters would offer her no more protection than any other Jew.

Esther fortified her strength with the prayers of her people. She requested all of the Jews, and all of her handmaidens in her own household, to fast, neither eating nor drinking for three days before she presented herself to the king. Esther knew that she could be condemned to death for entering the king's inner court without permission.

She took the courageous stance that "if I perish, let me perish," but I must have an audience with the king in an effort to save my people. Her integrity toward her family and her people spared their lives and caused Haman to be killed in the very gallows he had ordered built for Mordecai.

Omission of the truth can be an adversary to integrity in our homes. While there is undoubtedly some payoff for looking the other way, and feelings may be temporarily spared by living in conditions that we know are unhealthy for both our bodies and souls, eventually the truth will win out and the untruthful person will be found out. For some, it may mean holding on to the facade of a healthy marriage and refusing to seek counseling. For others, it may be the truth of their financial situations or some unethical decisions they make at work. We do have the power to choose truth, and doing so will foster a positive and healthy home atmosphere. Anything less than the truth shortchanges us, our family, and God.

Joanne and Rob have two daughters. Over the years, Joanne has chosen to be dishonest with Rob about their girls' behavior, which has caused him to lose trust and affection for his wife. They initially agreed that they would not allow their daughters to receive telephone calls from boys until they were thirteen years old or to date before each had reached the age of sixteen, respectively. The only boy in his own family, Rob had grown up in a home where he and his sisters had little parental discipline or structure. Home was a casual "open door" atmosphere with neighborhood boys in and out of the home with very little supervision. Rob's mom, who had maturity issues of her own, wanted to be seen as the cool mom that all the neighborhood kids wanted to be around.

Their home gained the reputation as the party house on the block, where underage kids could grab a cold beer from the refrigerator without fear of their parents being told. Rob's mom always said his father, who was usually working away from home, was too old-fashioned. Consequently, three of Rob's four sisters dropped out of high school, and two of them became pregnant before the age of sixteen. So, when he and Joanne saw their first tiny little girl outlined on a fuzzy ultrasound picture in the doctor's office, they committed to raising their children in a home where they would learn to love and value themselves. Unlike the home where he had been raised, his own children would be encouraged to develop into incredible people with a godly perspective and high self-esteem. He and Joanne would lovingly guide them together in their decision to date and build healthy relationships when the designated time arrived.

One day, Rob was summoned to his fifteen-year-old daughter's school to pick her up because she was ill. Panicked, not knowing what to expect, he nervously sat in the doctor's waiting room until her examination was complete. He was thankful to learn that she was suffering only from a twenty-four-hour bug for which several people waiting in the doctor's office were being treated. As the doctor advised him about which medications she could safely take to relieve the flu-like symptoms of her illness, he carefully warned Rob not to use anything that could adversely interact with the birth control medications his daughter was presently taking.

Visibly shaken, Rob was overwhelmed with shock

and disbelief, but the doctor's medical notes confirmed that Joanne had not only accompanied their daughter to the doctor's office but had requested and given written permission for the girl to receive the pills. Rob learned that both daughters had been receiving phone calls from boys since they were about twelve years old. Joanne had secretly thought it was "cute" that the girls were interested in boys at such a young age since she herself had been a tomboy during her adolescent years. She covered for them when Rob was around, pretending that their callers were girlfriends or classmates calling for assignments. Eventually, when their eldest daughter wanted to go out on a date at thirteen, Joanne announced that they were going out shopping; instead, she dropped her mature-looking daughter off at the local movie theater to meet a boy from school. The daughter's relationships had continually grown more intimate until Joanne, behind Rob's back, had taken her to the doctor for the pills. It was a major blow to their agreement to encourage their girls to wait and save that kind of intimacy for marriage.

This complete breakdown of trust and integrity in their home created a huge emotional divide between Rob and Joanne and brought them to the brink of divorce.

Rebekah, the wife of Isaac, favored her youngest son Jacob. In Genesis 27, she conspired with him to trick his father into giving him the birthright, which belonged to her eldest son, Esau. This act of deceit drove a wedge between the brothers and caused Esau to want to take Jacob's life. Jacob had to flee his beloved home and his family because he had stolen his brother's blessing. Esau's bitterness lasted for many years and Rebekah's duplicity in her home caused her family pain for generations.

Sometimes Christians mistakenly believe that smaller indiscretions do not count or cause harm in the home. For instance, asking your children or spouse to lie to bill collectors on your behalf does great harm to the credibility of your home. Furnishing your home with stolen or "hot" goods or buying bootlegged CDs, tapes, and videos to be enjoyed in your home shows a lack of integrity. We openly condemn the use of illegal drugs and yet some of us allow drug-dealing family members to live in our homes with us. We spend their cash and enjoy all the benefits that their drug money can buy. In Joshua 6:18 Joshua warns the people of God not to touch the accursed things. Accepting the accursed things would curse the camp—or home of the Israelites—and trouble it. It took the actions of only one among them, Achan, from the tribe of Judah, to incur the wrath of God. A battle that could have been won so easily was lost because of the accursed things hidden within the tent of Achan. So is it with our own homes. A home cannot be blessed and cursed at the same time. Ungodly and disobedient behaviors by a home's inhabitants can block the many blessings of God intended for or promised to them. How many of us are holding up our blessings because of the activities we allow within our homes?

- Know that home is a sacred space and it must be a haven to protect and respect the integrity of all who share it.
- Make a pact with yourself and all who dwell in your home to speak truth. Although truth should always be dispensed with wisdom, especially where children are concerned, it is essential to build your relationships on

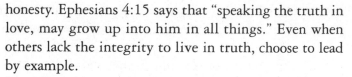
honesty. Ephesians 4:15 says that "speaking the truth in love, may grow up into him in all things." Even when others lack the integrity to live in truth, choose to lead by example.

- Provide children with the security of knowing that they can trust the adults in their homes. They will model adult behavior and they will test parental boundaries in the home while they are developing into young adults. When it serves them, children will find the weakest link in their home. Expect it and show them a united front.

Sylvia and her family moved to a new city when her husband's company relocated him to a new office. Although the move was good for his career, initially it came with no increase in his salary. The homes in the city cost considerably more than they had invested in their previous home. However, Sylvia felt confident that if they stuck to their agreement to purchase a reasonably priced modest home, she could continue to stay at home to care for her teenagers in their last years together before they flew the nest to create their own lives and personal spaces. When the decision was narrowed to three final choices, Sylvia knew that the smaller contemporary home that she admired on her first day of searching was just right for her family. Her husband, however, had been swayed by the children's pleas to purchase the more expensive home in a subdivision where many of their school friends lived. The house came complete with a country club membership and a whopping mortgage payment. Letting the final decision rest with Sylvia, she relented and gave in to the children's wishes. They purchased the home they could barely afford with the anticipation of future income increases with her husband's job.

Within months of moving into the house, the company moved the division of operations that Sylvia's husband managed out of the country. To protect his retirement and benefits package, he opted to stay with the company in a more subordinate position for considerably less money. Rather than making the obvious and sound decision of selling the house and purchasing a more affordable one, they made every effort to appease their children. While Sylvia began to search for work, she and her husband obtained advances on their credit cards to pay the mortgage and other bills. They did little to adjust their lifestyles. Unable to afford them, they still bought cars for their teenagers, paying exorbitant insurance rates because all the other parents in the neighborhood were doing so. Not only did Sylvia give up valuable time with her children, both she and her husband took on second jobs, sacrificing even more precious time in an effort to maintain the lie of living well. Before you sacrifice sound judgment for temporary gratification, keep in mind the following:

- Be willing to consider the home before the house. Create a lifestyle that is comfortable and affordable, thereby allowing time for loved ones.
- Stop trying to impress people, especially with what you really cannot afford.
- Learn to discern between your wants and your needs.
- Choose to take responsibility for the financial stability of your home.

- Never, ever allow fleeting emotional choices to trump sound financial decisions.
- Remember, living with integrity means living truthfully—both in your relationships and within your means.

~~~

A PRAYER OF CONSECRATION

Heavenly Father, Most High God, please consecrate my home. Reveal the accursed thing that may hinder relationship with You. Lord, let this home and everyone in it prosper in righteousness for Your glory. Impart Your wisdom to create a blessed place where Your Spirit can reign freely. Remove vanity, insincerity, and wickedness. Oh Lord, Who laid the foundation of the earth, I beseech You to lay the foundation of this home in Your holy Word. Let not this house be a rebellious one but instead one that is in subjection to Your will and to Your ways. Establish this home in sweetness and prudence, in honesty and integrity. Give understanding, for You are the source from which all blessings flow. We praise You and we bless Your name in this house forevermore. Amen.

Home Work

Put it in writing. Create a written contract or mission statement for yourself or your family and post it in a prominent place where it can be seen every day.

Take a literal inventory. Make a list of ways you can live more truthfully in your home. Do you lie about how much you spend on furnishings or clothing? Do you buy bootlegged products or allow illicit or immoral activity in your home (underage drinking and smoking, or illegal drug use, for example)?

Anything now in your home that was obtained by illegal activity should not remain in your home one more day. Haul it out to the Dumpster, or return it to its rightful owner. It doesn't matter how. Just get rid of it! Show God that you are serious about creating a home rooted in honesty and integrity.

Principle THIRTEEN

Stand Guard at the Gate and Be Careful Who Enters

Today, I will treat my blessed home as a place of refuge.
I will not compromise the standards of that refuge.
I will acknowledge my right to keep negative influences
and behavior away from the home I have worked
hard to create.

The dog is a lion in his own home.

PERSIAN PROVERB

*T*he wise King David had a remarkable understanding of this principle of standing guard at the gates of home. In Psalm 101:7 he says that anyone who was deceitful could not dwell in his home. The word *deceitful* is synonymous with words like dishonest, deceiving, lying, and faithless. Unfortunately, these words can describe many people we know. While we are charged above all else by God to love our neighbor as ourself, we need to have wisdom and discernment to know who we can allow into our inner sanctums.

This is surely one of the most freeing principles of all presented in this book, and yet I find so many people feel they need permission to eliminate strife in their own homes. A warped sense of obligation to people, mainly family and friends, convinces us to open our sacred spaces to those who are emotionally unhealthy and spiritually bankrupt. Sometimes they even seek to do us harm and destroy our homes.

Thomas and Nicole lived with their two young sons in a wonderful painstakingly restored arts and crafts cottage. It had become a favorite gathering place for their family and friends and a favorite place for Thomas, an advertising executive, to woo clients for his agency.

Another partner with the agency initiated an extramarital affair with a client and began to behave in an unconscionable manner with her at Thomas and Nicole's parties. Initially, they would exchange sly looks or slight touches of the hand. Soon, the partner failed to bring his wife to these gatherings and began displaying obvious signs of affection with "the other woman," openly hugging and kissing her. None of this escaped the curious minds of Thomas's sons, and after one such event, when all the guests had left, the boys began to fire a barrage of questions at their shocked parents. "Who is that woman?" "Where is his wife?" "Why does he kiss her the way you kiss Mommy?"

This was a defining moment for Thomas and Nicole, and they immediately began to reconsider the use of their home. They had allowed this behavior at one party too many for the sake of getting along with their business associates. The lifestyle they created for their family deeply encompassed their values, and their priority was to protect the developing hearts and spirits of their children. It was important to Thomas that he and Nicole be viewed by their sons as not supporting such behavior in their home. They decided that the standards they had set for their home would not be lowered for the sake of "sealing the deal." Its use is now relegated to entertaining loved ones and dear friends, those willing to respect the boundaries established in their home, not those who compromise their family values.

We must use similar discretion, even with the people we love. In the Book of Genesis, we know that Lot was a beloved nephew of Abraham. Abraham took Lot and Lot's household with him along his journey, and for years they lived and worked together, side by side. God blessed the home of Abraham, and Lot was blessed while he resided in that home. However, there came a time in their lives when these prosperous men began to have trouble in Abraham's home. In fact, they were so successful that the land could no longer sustain them. Their herdsmen who watched over their cattle began to bicker and fight about whose cattle should graze where. Abraham said to Lot in Genesis 13:8 "Let there be no strife, I pray thee, between me and thee, and between my herdsmen and thy herdsmen; for we be brethren." Abraham begged Lot to separate from his home, even giving him the pick of the choicest piece of land to relocate Lot's household. That speaks volumes about the importance to Abraham of having a peaceful home.

Elise and Geoffrey have only one son, Josh. All throughout his teen years, Josh was a joy to have at home. He loved school and he was heavily immersed in sports. He even managed to hold down a part-time job at the mall. His college years at the nearby university continued on successfully until his junior year, when he met his roommate, Greg. Greg was a smart kid but very flashy. He drove a European sports car and always seemed to have a pocketful of cash.

Josh became completely mesmerized by Greg's lifestyle, the girls, the parties, and the clothes. He was eager to accompany him on his business runs from time to time. It soon became apparent to Josh that Greg was dealing drugs, but Josh didn't really care, because Greg had such a great personality and he was very generous with him. Nearly six months later at one of Greg's parties, Josh tried a line of powdery white cocaine for the first time, and within months he, too, was using and dealing drugs.

Elise and Geoffrey were concerned for their son. They

did not know exactly what the problem was with Josh, but they were convinced that there indeed was one. Josh stopped attending classes, and after his parents received a letter from the university about his academic probation, they insisted that he move back home and enroll in a less stringent local community college. With the offer of free meals and no rent to pay, Josh jumped at the opportunity to move back home.

His father became increasingly suspicious that Josh was involved in some dubious activity. Josh's lack of interest in any of his old friends and the emaciated strangers who occasionally came knocking on their front door in the wee hours of the morning caused Geoffrey great concern. It was the small vials of rocklike substance tucked into Josh's pillowcase that confirmed his father's worst fears.

When they confronted him, Josh flew into a rage, accusing them of spying on him and treating him like a child. But Geoffrey stood firm and gave Josh an alternative. To continue to live in their home, he would immediately have to seek treatment and stop dealing drugs.

Josh saw his mother as the weak link in this supposed united front. He promised her that he was no longer using or dealing, and Elise believed him, although she continued to find wads of money stuffed into the pocket of his jeans when she pulled them from the dirty clothes hamper.

When Geoffrey felt that Josh was lying to them, Elise covered for him. Once in a while, when Geoffrey returned from business trips he was certain that he saw bruises on Elise's arm or shoulders that had not been there before. She always blamed her clumsiness, saying that she had fallen or bumped into some thing or another. Believing that Josh had become violent with his mother on several occasions, Geoffrey insisted that he leave their home right away. A frantic Elise, paralyzed by the fear of losing her son forever, told her husband that if he insisted on Josh leaving, she would leave, too. Resigned to pleasing his family, Geoffrey acquiesced, and against his better judgment, allowed Josh to stay.

One evening, beckoned to their shuttered windows by the sound of screeching sirens atop a convoy of police cars, Geoffrey and Elise were stunned to find their home surrounded by officers. One of Josh's regular customers was picked up on a felony burglary charge, stealing to support his drug habit. He gave Josh up as his dealer and the police had arrived at Geoffrey and Elise's door with a search warrant. Drugs were hidden everywhere. They were in a shoebox in Josh's closet, stuffed in the space between his mattress and box spring, and in a duffel bag stacked in the luggage organizer in the garage.

Not standing up for what was right in her home came at an incredible cost to Elise. According to the laws in their state, because of the large amount of drugs that Josh had stashed in their home, their house, the place where they thought they would live out their golden years, was seized. The home was held up in extensive legal wrangling for nearly two years under the threat of being sold, possibly leaving Elise and Geoffrey homeless. For the sake of keeping their son happy, Elise and Geoffrey sacrificed the sanctity of their home.

We all need to be diligent and aware of whom we allow to visit or stay in our homes. Remember:

- Keep your home a place of peace and refuge. Really know the people whom you choose to invite into your home, and make certain they will act respectfully toward your home and family.
- Be on guard for people who constantly criticize your home, no matter how politely they do it (e.g., "Your house is too formal." "The colors are too drab." "*I* wouldn't have chosen those drapes."). Keep out the negative emotions.
- Never compromise the standards you have set for your home and your lifestyle for "business" purposes. No one is required to shelter family members who might be breaking the law.
- Be leery of anyone who is willing to risk your home and happiness for their own selfish motives.
- Do not allow pressure from family or acquaintances to force you into allowing someone into your home who should not be there, for any reason.

Acknowledge your right to say no!

- Never, ever, allow unsavory people—relatives included—into your home if you or your children could be at risk or in danger. You have no obligation to toxic or dangerous people. This is a valuable lesson that your children must learn. Sometimes at work and in other public situations, we are forced to interact with people we may not necessarily like, but we must draw the line at home. Exercise your power to choose.
- Never live in a home where you or your children are subjected to abuse. It is better to live peaceably in a

shack than to live in a mansion with the constant fear
of violence and violation.

Seek God for Divine Wisdom.

- Pray, pray, and then pray some more. Life is, as Job said,
full of troubles. You will inevitably deal with some
struggles in your own home. Acknowledge that you do
not have the answer to every challenge that might over-
whelm you, but with God's help you can survive and
overcome any struggle. Ask Him to guide your decisions, especially when they are "tough-love" ones.

Home Work

If you are unsure whether someone should or should not be invited into your home, use this checklist as a guideline to help you decide.

PROFILE SHEET

Does he or she:

1. *Constantly criticize your home or insist that they would have done things differently?*
2. *Bring other disrespectful or unsavory people along for visits to your home?*
3. *Become drunken, disorderly, or verbally abusive to you or your family?*
4. *Make you feel uncomfortable leaving your purse, wallet, or valuables in full view?*
5. *Make unsolicited and uncomfortable sexual remarks toward you or your spouse?*
6. *Make you feel uncomfortable when they interact with your children?*
7. *Leave you emotionally drained after each visit?*
8. *Become the focus of arguments between you and your spouse after a visit?*
9. *Cause you to have to justify their bad behavior to others who have been made uncomfortable?*
10. *Use illegal drugs or engage in criminal behavior of any sort?*

Now exercise your power to choose!

Principle FOURTEEN

Celebrate

Today, I will celebrate victories big and small.

And thou shalt rejoice in every good thing which the Lord thy God hath given unto thee, and unto thine house.

DEUTERONOMY 26:11

*C*elebration is an important part of our lives. It provides memorable milestones for special events we will cherish forever. What better way is there to reward ourselves for creating a blessed home than to celebrate whenever we can?

King David understood the art of celebration. The Bible says that when the Ark of the Covenant was being carried into the city of David, he stood outside and danced. The king danced right out of his praise garments.

Moreover, in the story of the Prodigal Son, the wise father and king threw a party upon the return of his son. He commanded his servants to kill and prepare a fatted calf and "Let us eat and be merry." The king obviously understood that celebrating his child, even though the son had been in error, would make him feel loved, accepted, and important to the family.

The human brain is incredible in how it records extraordinary events, be they good or bad, forever. Think about it. Most of us can remember in amazing detail the day we received that bike we longed for as a kid or a special Christmas or birthday party.

Jennifer takes celebrating seriously in her home. She goes the extra mile to make "happy memories" for her brood. Practically every holiday is acknowledged with her seasonal tableaus and her ever-changing tableware displays. For no occasion at all, she floats love notes attached to helium balloons into her children's rooms. Jennifer memorializes every birthday and anniversary in some special way. When one of her children does some outstanding thing in school, church, or sports, she makes them king or queen for the day, indulging them at home with their favorite foods and allowing them to select their favorite video or fun family activity to do together. They have dedicated space on one of the walls in their family room as the "winners wall"—a constantly changing display of candid photographs of triumphant moments in each of their lives.

A truly blessed home is one that provides the backdrop for your most memorable moments.

- Host a dinner party or a surprise baby shower. Throw a party for no reason at all!
- Fellowship with people who share mutual love and respect; this is a great way to stay upbeat and excited about life.
- Renew your wedding vows at home in your yard, poolside, or in your formal flower garden.
- Don't sweat it! Put together a party in an instant. Order Chinese take-out or plan an informal barbecue to feed the masses without much effort.

Celebrate the small victories, too!

- Allow the family to acknowledge Mom receiving a promotion, a child getting an A on a report card or learning to tie a shoe, or Dad exceeding a sales goal at work.

• Encourage your family to share their stories of daily victories with one another at dinnertime or bedtime.

Taking careful note of how his father and I indulge each other during Mother's Day and Father's Day, my son decreed that he and his sister should be allowed to celebrate Sibling Day. On their appointed day, they are especially pleasant to one another. They play together, watch videos together, and make cards for each other. Ray and I take the children shopping separately to buy a surprise gift for the other sibling with money each has saved in their piggy banks. This celebrated event is a perfect time to update their annual sibling portrait, followed by a trip to the local Dairy Queen to split a huge ice cream sundae.

Be original in your choice of events to celebrate. Don't just wait for a popular holiday; create an occasion that is unique to your family. Give your special day a name and create your own traditions around your holiday. Go all out with food and decorations.

Fourteen-year-old fraternal twins, Kyle and Kerri, began to use this principle at an early age. This dynamic duo are avid swimmers who love to host pool parties. Born in the month of December, they were never able to celebrate their birthday poolside because of the harsh northeastern climate during the winter months. When the kids were seven, Kerri boldly announced that she and Kyle would be celebrating their "half" birthday point in the middle of the summer. Impressed by the twins' creativity, their parents enthusiastically embraced the idea, and their mom set out to plan a "half"-themed party. She found a local baker to create a special cake. One-half of the cake was chocolate, Kyle's favorite, and the other half was vanilla, Kerri's choice. Each child got to have half the menu and decorations filled with his and her favorite foods and colors, respectively, and the guest list reflected exactly half of his and her best friends. At first, some thought the idea of the yearly "half" birthday parties to be a little unusual, but this family's creativity has made every celebration a delightful event. In fact, family and friends look forward to receiving their invitations just to see what new "half" ideas will be incorporated into the next party.

Home Work

Find reasons to celebrate something special every month. Below is a list of suggestions but be innovative and create your own ideas too!

Sibling Day
Pet Birthdays
Pamper Me Day
Family Fun Day
TV Free Day
Mom and Sons
    Dinner

Best Friends Brunch
Garden Party
Pool Party
Dad and Daughters
    Dinner
Good Deed Day

Art Appreciation Day
Parents' Date Night
Worry-Free Day
Neighborhood Block
    Party

Add several of your own ideas for personal celebrations.

_____

_____

_____

Don't wait for special moments to happen. Create them!

- *Encourage your spouse to take a midday Saturday nap with you.*
- *Let the kids snuggle with you on the sofa while you all watch their favorite silly movie.*
- *Allow family members to help select and plant their favorite flowers in the yard. Children derive great pleasure from seeing the things that they plant in pots or in a garden thrive and grow.*
- *Enjoy the blessed home you have created whenever you can with those you cherish.*

Afterword

I hope that by the time you have reached this page, God has touched your heart to consider the way in which you are choosing to live. The idea for *Sanctuary* came as a result of much fasting, praying, and seeking God for His wisdom. I asked God to make me a vessel to create a work that would be of use to His people.

It is my desire that you reflect on the spiritual condition of your sacred space as you endeavor to create a home that is beautiful and unique. The home is a powerful entity! Don't look to please your neighbors. Strive to do what is pleasing and acceptable in the eyes of the Lord. Wise people, the Bible says, use their hands to build up their homes.

It is a tremendous blessing for me to share with you what God has imparted in my spirit, and I encourage every one of you to live well and be *blessed in your Sanctuary!*

Acknowledgments

Thank You, God, for inspiring and entrusting me with an idea and allowing me to see it through to fruition.

Thank you, Ray, for being the wonderful man you are. I am grateful that you were my destiny, and I appreciate all of your love, patience, kindness, support, and encouragement. Thank you for being a great father to our children and making the shared responsibility of parenting a joy.

Braeden Alexander and Brinn Elizabeth, I thank God for you daily. I thank you both for choosing me as your mother and allowing me to have the most awesome experience that a woman can have on this planet. You two inspire me to be more and to grow deeper every day of my life. I love you both unconditionally.

Special thanks to my siblings, Cathy, Craig, and Deshazor, for supporting all my endeavors. To Ramona Everett for being who you are in my family's life and Janice Grady for believing in the possibilities. Thank you, Maureen and Tim Laniak, for your prayers and Audrey and Oliver Brown for being the best possible friends in every way. To Alice White for being my sister and having my back. Uncle Tang, thank you for always showing us that you loved us no matter what. Dia', Breyan, Destiny, Taylor, Kyla, and Lawrence William-Edward, thank you for allowing me to love you. Live in truth and love!

Sister-friend, Coach Kelly Jones-Waller, thank you for pushing me toward my goal and not letting me give up. Thank you for reminding me whose child I am.

Pastor Malachi Haines and my beautiful sister in Christ, Gwen Haines, I can never thank you enough for your counsel, your prayers, and the generosity of your spirit. Continue to be "steadfast, immovable, and always abounding in the work of the Lord." My Upper Room family, continue to press toward the mark and prepare for greatness. I love you all.

Thank you, Michelle Andrea Bowen, for following the lead of the Lord. Thank you, Denise Stinson and the Walk Worthy Press family, for allowing me to spread a good word. Dr. Pat MacEnulty and Irene Prokop, thank you for your time and your talent. You were a blessing to this project.

Reading Group Guide

The author has already provided "Home Work" with each chapter. Use the following questions and topics to supplement what is already supplied for consideration in the book.

Dreams

1. In Scripture, the word *house* encompasses two key meanings: the physical structure that a person or group inhabits (i.e., housing) and the person or group who inhabits that home (i.e., household). When Joshua swore "As for me and my house, we will serve the Lord," he was referring to his household—his family and all those dependent on his family for a livelihood. When David dreamed of building a "house for God"—the temple— God's response was to prioritize building David's house—his dynasty—first. When you consider seeking a blessing on your house, how is your household encompassed by that prayer? Consider how your dreams, plans, and decisions concerning your *housing* affect your *household*.

2. Whether you are anticipating your first home, your fourth, or your fifteenth, you have dreams about what that home will be like. What factors figure into those dreams? Why? Don't neglect to consider the following:

- **Location, location, location!** Think about the geography of your home search, especially as it relates to the proximity of your circle of support (family, friends, church); critical or desirable service and supplies (medical care, schooling, food, fuel, public transportation, thoroughfares); frequent destinations (work, school, medical facilities, ministry sites); cultural or recreational resources (parks, museums, theaters, sporting venues, children's entertainment).

- **Won't you be my neighbor?** Think about the village in which you prefer to live. Are you a city or country mouse—or do you prefer the middle ground of the suburbs? What are the pros and cons of each? Do you enjoy your space, or do you crave the bustle of other people—or both in varying proportions? What population and population density are encompassed by this neighborhood? What are the demographics of your ideal neighborhood? Do you crave racial or socioeconomic solidarity—or diversity? Investigate the reputations of the community's schools, and its sanitation and emergency services. Find out what the taxes are—and what is included in them!

- **What I want vs. what I need:** Give detailed consideration to what kind of home you *want* at this time in your life and what kind of home you *need*. The two are not necessarily the same. You may want a modest but modern, three-story townhome in a cooperative community in the sultry South, where you don't have to worry about landscaping or dozens of rooms to keep clean or the cold harsh winters of the Great Lakes region where you grew up. But your household may require a sprawling, century-old ranch house in the Southwest, where your young child with allergies and your aging father with a walker can share space indoors and enjoy room to roam outside.

• **Write the vision—even if it is twofold:** Now that you have recognized the difference between your desire and your need, write down both visions—and commit them each to God. Be detailed: square footage and acreage; number of bedrooms and baths; modern conveniences or old-world charms; multilevel or ranch style; closets and storage space; basement and/or attic, finished or unfinished; garage and/or shed; driveway and sidewalks. Think about practicalities such as plumbing, windows, roof, and appliances. Do you want to design your own or identify a fixer-upper that needs your TLC? Do you prefer new construction, or a place with a history? If the latter, how much history? The more specific you are about the visions, the more awed and grateful you will be when God brings that vision to pass!

Decisions

3. Once the dream is clear, you are faced with some decisions. How long are you willing or able to wait for the dream? Do you believe God is calling you to hold out for the desire of your heart—or do you sense the Spirit

saying, "Accept this for now and trust the rest to me"? Both decisions are intensely spiritual and personal.

4. Proverbs reminds us that there is wisdom in a multitude of counselors. A common adage is that two heads are better than one. It is also true that there can be too many cooks in a kitchen! Whom will you consult in making the necessary decisions related to your housing? Don't forget that renting or buying a home is not only a matter of faith; it is also a decision that can involve a tangle of attached strings. Seek spiritual counsel—and legal and financial advice. Ask God for wisdom in choosing *all* of your advisors, from a real estate agent to an attorney to a loan officer to a management company.

Decorations

5. You have dreamed your dreams and made your decision—and now you stand on the threshold of your new home. Or perhaps, you have decided against a new home at this time, and you are resolved to do *new* work on your *old* home! Consider your space carefully and again, think about your wants versus your needs.

• **Not just outward appearances:** Keep in mind the biblical exhortation about God's concern more with the spirit inside than with the outer dressing. A beautiful home may house a cold or dying spirit. A crowded and cluttered house may harbor the warmth of hospitality and peace. Are you as effective a steward of your household as you are of your house? Does your home reflect the spirit and personality of your family?

• **Something old, something new:** What things do you enjoy surrounding yourself with? Do you love the newest trend in decorating, something with sleek, modern lines and stark colors; or are you a traditionalist who prefers country style and wicker? Do you adore antiques or love knowing that no one but you has planted her hands on that spotless piece of furniture? Consider also how changeable your likes and dislikes are. Do you like to build a nest and settle in for the long haul, secure in having what is beloved and familiar around you? Or are you one who revels in novelty and change, craving something new to see, touch, smell, and taste? Take those personality preferences into consideration as you decorate your home and make responsible investments.

• **Kids will be kids:** If you have young children in your home (or are planning to add some in the near future), be mindful of that as you design your home's interior. Safety is the key issue: How safe are children around your possessions—and how safe are your possessions around children? It is possible to have nice things and toddlers in the same home, but there is a price tag on that combination. Count the cost—monetary and in peace of mind—now, so you don't regret it later.

Doors

6. Shakespeare wrote, "All the world's a stage," and in life as in theater, entrances and exits are important. Does that artwork come in? Does that story go out? Does that

language make an entrance? Does that attitude make an exit? Do we make solo or group exits? What caregivers or influences are permitted entrance? Now that you are in your home, give prayerful consideration to what and who comes in and goes out of your house—and household.

7. Throughout Scripture, God's people are urged to practice hospitality. However, because each person is unique—in personality and gifts—each house (and household) will welcome others differently into the sanctuary of home. Ask these questions, among others, about the opening of your doors:

• **To whom should the door be open?** To whom will you grant entry—only friends and family, or also strangers and enemies? At issue is not only the question of hospitality and generosity, but also that of safety and wisdom.

• **On what occasions should the door be open?** Will your home have a revolving door, open to guests whenever the impulse strikes? Or will you make your hospitality special, even sacred in some way, by choosing specific events for which to welcome people—holidays or meals or a monthly fellowship?

• **Which doors should you open?** Which parts of your home will be public territory? Will you serve them in the dining room or welcome them in the kitchen? Will every inch of your house be offered to your guests, or will you reserve special rooms for entertaining? If the latter, will the rooms be formal or informal spaces?

• **When should the door be open?** Will the door be open at all times of day and night or only during "business hours"? Will you close the door on specific days that might be reserved for family, cleaning, or rest? Will you have a special day, weekend, or time frame set aside for entertaining—or will you throw open your doors without notice?

• **Why will you open your doors?** To celebrate or provide refuge? For fun or ministry? Out of a sense of Christian responsibility or because you are the quintessential extrovert? Do you enjoy having people around and sharing your space? Or does company stress you out and make you long for solitude?

• **Whether to open the door—or not?** Will there be times when you shut the doors of your home? Might you choose to shut out certain influences, at least for a season? Or will it be a time of refuge or intimate fellowship—when you, as an individual or as a family, just need some "me/us time"?

8. Because of the physical and spiritual significance of doors, seriously consider having a "Home Blessing" ceremony in your new or renewed home. Many pastors or church leaders are willing to visit a home and say a prayer of blessing over it, even anointing the doorway(s) with oil as a sign of sanctification. If your church does not have such a convention in place, consider introducing the idea to the leadership, or invite a trusted friend of faith to share in a ceremony with you.

About the Author

PAMELA J. BAILEY is a graduate of South Carolina State University with a bachelor of science degree in Marketing. She is currently the co-founder and owner of Graybail International, LLC, and The Gilded Nest, a spiritually themed giftware and home accessory business.

Pamela is devoted to helping people live well in whatever circumstance they may find themselves. She is a dynamic motivational speaker who is passionate about her work. Her candid and honest approach allows her to appeal to people across a broad spectrum as she speaks to audiences, teaching these principles. Her greatest accomplishment is creating her own sanctuary, which she shares with her best friend, her husband, C. Ray Bailey and their two children.

Please share your response to the book and the impact it has made in your home with the author. To book the author for speaking engagements, workshops, or for all other correspondence, please send written requests to:

Pamela J. Bailey/Sanctuary
P.O. Box 542
Monroe, North Carolina 28111

NONFICTION TITLES ALSO AVAILABLE FROM
WALK WORTHY PRESS

**What Matters Most: Ten Lessons in
Living Passionately from the Song of Solomon,**
by RENITA J. WEEMS

The *#1 Essence* bestselling author draws inspiration from the Bible's Song of Solomon to examine the role passion plays in women's lives.

**I Say a Prayer for Me:
One Woman's Life of Faith and Triumph,**
by STANICE ANDERSON

God's faithfulness is displayed in one woman's journey through addiction, tragedy, and pain.

**Daughters of the King: Finding Victory Through
Your God-Given Personal Style,**
by GAIL M. HAYES, PhD

This book celebrates the individual style and beauty of women and helps move them beyond their "church lady" identity crisis in a fun and empowering way.

**Lift Up Your Hands:
Raise Your Praise and Get Lost in God,**
by GLORIA P. PRUETT

Minister Pruett helps readers focus and uncover their personal, plentiful reasons to give God praise.

God's Word for the Unmarried Believer,
by the Editors of Walk Worthy Press

A down-to-earth and humorous devotional to encourage those who are single to delve deeper into God's plan for their lives.

Reading Groups for African American
Christian Women Who Love God and Like to Read.

BE A PART OF
GLORY GIRLS READING GROUPS!

THESE EXCITING BI-MONTHLY READING GROUPS ARE FOR THOSE SEEKING FELLOWSHIP WITH OTHER WOMEN WHO ALSO LOVE GOD AND ENJOY READING.

For more information about GLORY GIRLS, to connect with an established group in your area, or to become a group facilitator, go to our Web site at **www.glorygirlsread.net** or click on the Praising Sisters logo at **www.walkworthypress.net**.

WHO WE ARE

GLORY GIRLS is a national organization made up of primarily African American Christian women, yet it welcomes the participation of anyone who loves the God of the Bible and likes to read.

OUR PURPOSE IS SIMPLE

- To honor the Lord with <u>what we read</u>—and have a good time doing it!

- To provide an atmosphere where readers can seek fellowship with other book lovers while encouraging them in the choices they make in Godly reading materials.

- To offer readers fresh, contemporary, and entertaining yet scripturally sound fiction and nonfiction by talented Christian authors.

- To assist believers and nonbelievers in discovering the relevancy of the Bible in our contemporary, everyday lives.